THE PILLAR
of the TRUTH

Douglas Wilson, *The Pillar of the Truth: A Commentary on the Pastoral Epistles (1 Timothy, 2 Timothy, and Titus)*
Copyright ©2016 by Douglas Wilson

Published by Canon Press
P. O. Box 8729, Moscow, Idaho 83843
800-488-2034 | www.canonpress.com

Cover design by James Engerbretson
Interior design by Valerie Anne Bost
Printed in the United States of America

Unless otherwise indicated, all Scripture quotations are from the King James Version. All Bible quotations marked ESV are from the English Standard Version copyright ©2001 by Crossway Bibles, a division of Good News Publishers. Used by permission.

Names: Wilson, Douglas, 1953- author.
Title: The pillar of the truth : the pastoral epistles (1 Timothy, 2 Timothy, and Titus) / by Douglas Wilson.
Description: Moscow : Canon Press, 2016. | Series: Canon Commentaries ; 1
Identifiers: LCCN 2016027446 | ISBN 9781944503505 (pbk.)
Subjects: LCSH: Bible. Pastoral epistles--Commentaries.
Classification: LCC BS2735.53 .W55 2016 | DDC 227/.83077--dc23
LC record available at https://lccn.loc.gov/2016027446

17 18 19 20 21 22 23   10 9 8 7 6 5 4 3 2 1

THE PILLAR
of the TRUTH

A COMMENTARY ON
THE PASTORAL EPISTLES
(1 TIMOTHY, 2 TIMOTHY, AND TITUS)

DOUGLAS WILSON

canonpress
Moscow, Idaho

CONTENTS

INTRODUCTION

In the typological relationship of Old Testament to New Testament, we have to remember the importance of terrain. Mountain ranges answer to mountain ranges, great rivers to great rivers, canyons to canyons, and of course, ordinary meadows to ordinary meadows.

A great mountain would be something like the relationship of Adam to the second Adam (Rom. 5:14, 18; 1 Cor. 15:22, 45). The typology of the tabernacle answers to the heavenly antitype (Heb. 9:12), as well as to its future antitype in the Christian Church (Heb. 9:10). The Holy of Holies in the old covenant is a perfect cube, the same shape as the New Jerusalem coming down out of Heaven like a bride adorned for her husband (Rev. 21:9).

When we are given space to breathe, as we sometimes are, this is not because the typology switch has been turned off. Rather, it is because once issues of great moment have been settled, it becomes necessary to turn at some point to the day-to-day business of governance. We sometimes mistakenly put the sheen of antiquity on events from centuries ago, as though the apostle Paul somehow didn't have to put his sandals on in the morning. I recall how startled I was while reading a biography of John Chrysostom, when I came across a reference to the minutes of one of their Church meetings. *Minutes?*

In the pastoral epistles, the apostle Paul has, near the end of his life, turned to the crucial business of institutionalization. He knows that the institution of the Church is inevitable, and he, more than anyone, knows the temptations that will beset that institution. But the fact that temptations will necessarily come to the best-planned institution is no argument for planning the whole thing poorly. If the temptations finally overwhelm the poor little ecclesiastical functionaries, and they go the way of all flesh, a well-planned set of institutional blueprints (as we find in the pastorals) will provide the marching orders for the inevitable reformers. If the Temple falls into disrepair, we may still take heart—a copy of Deuteronomy remains in its shambles of a library, and Josiah will find it.

Nevertheless, despite this focus on the institution, we still see an awareness of typological transition. The Church was about to enter the period that answered to the books of Joshua and Judges. They had come to the end of their forty years in the wilderness—the time between the Ascension of Jesus and the destruction of the Temple. During those forty years a number of remarkable things had happened to both Israel and the Church. Both had extraordinary government (Moses and the apostles), both had ordinary government taking shape (elders and elders), both had to withstand challenges to their extraordinary rulers (Korah and Paul's enemies), and so on. Given the circumstances, it is not surprising that the typology we see has to do with government and rule.

We can see this awareness in how the Old Testament is quoted and applied in the pastorals. The first citation has to do with the payment of ministers. "For the Scripture saith, thou shalt not muzzle the ox that treadeth out the corn. And, The labourer is worthy of his reward" (1 Tim. 5:18; cf. 1 Cor. 9:9). This is a citation from Deut. 25:4. The second part of the verse is from Luke 10:7, cited alongside Deuteronomy as "Scripture." We can see how, within the space of the first generation of Christians, one of the apostles is talking to the elders about their future budgets. Not only so, but a passage from one of the gospels is cited authoritatively as Scripture, right alongside Deuteronomy.

The next quoted verse sets up the threshold for entertaining charges against elders (1 Tim. 5:19) by quoting the requirement of Deuteronomy 19:15. Everything must be established in the mouth of two or three witnesses. This is another procedural governmental requirement, one essential to a healthy institution.

It is not possible to have a biblical form of government without it being challenged by somebody. A naive person might assume that the more biblical the form of government was, the less likely a challenge would be. This is not at all the case. Moses had to fight off a challenge to his

authority in the wilderness, and Paul, who knew exactly what that felt like, quoted Moses from the episode of
Korah's rebellion. Moses said, as did Paul:

> Nevertheless the foundation of God standeth sure,
> having this seal, The Lord knoweth them that are his.
> (2 Tim. 2:19a)

And this was the situation that Paul identified with.

> And they gathered themselves together against Moses
> and against Aaron, and said unto them, Ye take too
> much upon you, seeing all the congregation are holy,
> every one of them, and the Lord is among them:
> wherefore then lift ye up yourselves above the con-
> gregation of the Lord? And when Moses heard it, he
> fell upon his face: And he spake unto Korah and unto
> all his company, saying, Even to morrow the Lord will
> shew who are his, and who is holy; and will cause him
> to come near unto him: even him whom he hath cho-
> sen will he cause to come near unto him. This do; Take
> you censers, Korah, and all his company; And put fire
> therein, and put incense in them before the Lord to
> morrow: and it shall be that the man whom the Lord
> doth choose, he shall be holy: ye take too much upon
> you, ye sons of Levi. And Moses said unto Korah, Hear,
> I pray you, ye sons of Levi: Seemeth it but a small
> thing unto you, that the God of Israel hath separated
> you from the congregation of Israel, to bring you near
> to himself to do the service of the tabernacle of the
> Lord, and to stand before the congregation to minister

unto them? And he hath brought thee near to him, and all thy brethren the sons of Levi with thee: and seek ye the priesthood also? For which cause both thou and all thy company are gathered together against the Lord: and what is Aaron, that ye murmur against him? (Num. 16:3–11)

The follow-up comment in that same verse—"And, let every one that nameth the name of Christ depart from iniquity" (2 Tim. 2:19b)—contains echoes of Proverbs 16:6.

A bit later in 2 Timothy, we find out the name of one of Paul's adversaries. We are not told a great deal about him, only his name, the fact that he was a coppersmith and that he did Paul great damage. We do not know if he was within the Church or outside it, but given the nature of Paul's concerns in this letter, I would be inclined to mark him down as a New Testament Korah.

Alexander the coppersmith did me much evil: the Lord reward him according to his works. (2 Tim. 4:14)

When the judgment of the Lord falls, it will fall on those both within the covenant and outside it—" Also unto thee, O Lord, belongeth mercy: for thou renderest to every man according to his work" (Ps. 62:12).

At the same time, for all the work that Paul is doing in preparation for "the Church as institution," we can clearly see that he is not resigning himself to an inevitable downgrade when it comes to holiness. If institutionalization is inevitable, then holiness must be able to take an institutional form. God is the one "Who gave himself for us, that he might redeem us from all iniquity, and purify unto himself a peculiar people, zealous of good works" (Titus 2:14). This appears to be a collage of Ps. 130:8, Ezek. 37:23, and Deut. 14:2.

One of the most important things we can learn from Scripture is how to see ourselves accurately in the story in which we find ourselves. What story is God telling, and how does it concern us? For busy pastors, whose lives are filled with counseling, committee meetings, small town politics, and more, the hard-headed typological lessons of the pastorals can be a great encouragement.

AUTHORSHIP

A s we begin our study of what are called the pastoral epistles, it is important to contextualize them.
Reconstructing the chronology of the New Testament, we
may conclude that Paul was probably imprisoned in Rome
twice. The first is found at the end of the book of Acts, after
which he was released, and during which time he wrote 1
Timothy and Titus (c. A.D. 62–66). When he was imprisoned again (at the end of which time he was executed), he
wrote 2 Timothy. It is fashionable for many modern scholars to dispute the Pauline authorship of the epistles, and,
also sadly, it is common for more conservative scholars
to argue for the Pauline authorship without reference to
chapter one, verse one. "Paul, an apostle . . . " If we believe
in the inspiration of Scripture, as we do, it follows that we

should believe God is not lying to us. If the letters claim to be from Paul, this is a truth claim. As a truth claim, if it is the Word of God, it needs to be *true*.

At the same time, we need to interact with the reasons given for denying Pauline authorship. After all, liberal commentaries don't deny Pauline authorship because "We're liberals, and that's just what we do." The trick here is to give the question the time it deserves without giving it the time of day. That said, here are some of the basic reasons why it is thought by some that Paul did not write these letters.[1]

First is *the historical problem*.[2] Scholars have sometimes had trouble bringing together the historical narrative of Acts and the historical tidbits in the pastorals. Specifically in Titus, there is a trip to Nicopolis. Many have tried, but most scholars agree that it is impossible to fit the historical facts given in the pastorals within the framework of the book of Acts.

Then there is *the ecclesiastical problem*. This argument goes along the line that the structure of the Church given in the Timothys and Titus is much too advanced for the time of Paul. This view has four main tenets. 1) Paul was not really into organizing the Church. Paul was more into an organic organization (as in Corinth and Philippi), not the rigid organization of the pastorals. 2) Elders in the

1 In this section on Pauline authorship that follows, I am interacting with modern scholarly opinions on Timothy, including those found in *The New Bible Dictionary*, ed. J.D. Douglas (Grand Rapids: Eerdmans, 1962).

2 Also, in keeping with the wider debate on inerrancy, I've used the common names for these "problems" (so of course the names and organization of these topics are not original to me).

pastorals are seen as "tradition-bearers," passing on the tradition. If this is the case, how could Paul set up such a system before the tradition was fixed? The function of these elders is seen as being too advanced for the time of Paul. 3) This third point applies to 1 Timothy, but not to Titus. This is the feeling expressed by the author that he is dealing with an established Church. This hint is found in 1 Tim. 3:6, where Timothy is warned against appointing new converts as elders. This implies the existence of older converts, i.e., an established Church. The opposite impression is given in the letter to Titus, who appears to be starting from scratch. 4) Titus and Timothy seem to be in the position of a monarchical episcopate, found in the early second century. Not only were they elders, they appointed other elders and apparently were over them in authority. 5) A final objection given is the fact of the heresies countered in the Pastorals. These particular heresies are assumed to have been much stronger in the second century. At their peak, as it were.

The third issue for Pauline authorship is *the doctrinal problem*—the emphasis on "doctrine" is seen as not being Pauline. An example would be the absence of characteristic Pauline thoughts, which have been described as "the Fatherhood of God, the mystic union of the believer with Christ and the work of the Holy Spirit." The emphasis in the pastorals is that, now that the doctrine has been established, let us hold to it steadfastly. It has shifted from "this is the faith" to "keep the faith."

Fourth, we find *the linguistic problem*. In the pastorals are a large number of words unique to the New Testament.

Also, there are a lot of words shared with non-Pauline books and *not* shared with Paul's other works. This is not limited to vocabulary, but includes style. It is also maintained that the vocabulary of the Pastorals is a vocabulary of common use in the second century. This is asserted because of a comparison with the writings of the apostolic Fathers, apologists, and even second-century writers who were not Christian. Out of all the problems mentioned above, the most important ones for many adherents of a non-Pauline authorship are these linguistic considerations.

This view would probably hold that a scribal Paulbot of the early second century came up with the pastorals to meet some of the practical needs of his own time. The inclusion of genuine Pauline fragments and phrases from Paul's other letters supplies the feeling that Paul wrote them. This fellow, whoever he was, was a fine mimic, imitating Paul in everything except his dedication to telling the truth. This would also account for their early and full acceptance by the Church as being letters from Paul.

Here are some suggested answers to these supposed problems. First, *the historical problem* assumes a great deal from silence. Acts does not say that Paul was ever released; it ends with him in prison. This is tantamount to saying that if it isn't recorded in Acts, it can't be considered authentic. But since Acts leaves out *many* details of Paul's life (2 Cor. 11), this can't be considered a hard and fast rule at all. Paul lived many years that were not recorded in Acts. It needs to be underlined that there is *no* evidence that Paul did not do any further missionary work. This leaves wide open the possibility that he did. Can we proceed from possibility to probability?

Why was Paul sent to Rome in the first place? The answer is that he had appealed to Caesar. In Acts 26, Agrippa states that Paul could have been set free had he not so appealed. We have no reason to think that Festus disagreed. Acts 25:20 is clear that Festus was thrown for a loss due to the religious nature of the charges against him. Unless further charges were brought against Paul (and none are mentioned), it seems that the normal course of Roman justice would have resulted in Paul being released after the close of Acts. This means that there was a second Roman imprisonment, one that provides a background for the history of the pastorals. There is no reason Paul could not have gone to Nicopolis after his release.

Another point in favor of the second imprisonment theory is the abrupt close to the book of Acts. Opponents of the second imprisonment theory can say that it is strange that Luke does not mention Paul's release and renewed missionary efforts. But if this theory is *not* true, it is stranger still that Luke did not mention Paul's martyrdom. So, then, the strange ending of Acts is in favor of the release theory. The burden of proof lies with the opponents of Pauline authorship, and the argument from historical silence is inadequate.

To answer *the ecclesiastical problem*, it is necessary to point out that it is *not* true that Paul was disinterested in Church organization. It is likely that Paul himself appointed elders when he and Barnabas were on their way back from the first missionary journey (in south Galatia). When

Paul was passing through Miletus in Acts 20:17, he sent for the elders in the Ephesian Church. This leaves open the possibility that Paul had in fact appointed them. But it tells us at a minimum that there was an elder-system set up during Paul's prime, and Paul was involved with those said elders. Paul mentions "pastors and teachers" in Ephesians, who were likely in the position of elders. The bishops and deacons of Philippi would support the references to the elder-system in the Acts.

Not only is it unbiblical to believe that the elder-system is a later development than Paul, to do so also rests on two misunderstandings. First, it assumes that the main function of an elder is to transmit the tradition. This probably became *more* true in the later stages of the Church, but we should not say that Paul could not have foreseen this need. To argue this is to maintain that Paul was one shortsighted individual. The second misunderstanding is to think that by the end of Paul's life, he still had no conception of a body of doctrine that he wanted passed on. Paul must have seen that the survival of the Church would depend on the tradition-bearers. The pastorals clearly reflect a Paul open to this challenge.

Also, the heresies in the pastorals are not to be refuted (as in Colossians), but ignored. They are dangerous, true enough, but more than that, they are useless. The full-blown Gnostic heresy of the second century would have required refutation, and not be merely dismissed as "godless chatter."

Then there is *the doctrinal problem*. The main charge to be considered is that Paul's dynamic faith has become "*the* faith" in the pastorals, i.e., the faith to be handed down and steadfastly kept. But Paul also spoke of "the faith" in Ephesians 4:5, Philippians 1:27, and Colossians 2:7 (as others have also pointed out).

It is also charged that "Paul" leaves out the typical Pauline thrust of the mystical union in Christ. But qualities "in Christ" are mentioned nine times in the pastorals. Although Paul usually applies the phrase to persons, not qualities, using that distinction to show the absence of union with Christ is pretty close to hair-splitting. Disembodied qualities do not float around without persons.

No major case could be made that the words "grace" and "justified" have had their meaning changed at all. In Titus 3:5, the traditional Pauline view on salvation shines forth clearly. Nothing in the pastorals would disagree with Paul on the great subject of grace.

So it is with the Holy Spirit. A case cannot be made from the infrequent mentioning of Him. (Colossians and 2 Thessalonians mention the Holy Spirit one time only.) What mention there is, Paul would be in hearty agreement with. Nor can it be claimed that God is too far removed for Paul. See Titus 2:11, 3:4, and 1:3. God in these passages is *not* remote.

And last, there is *the linguistic problem.* There are two issues here—the problem of vocabulary and the problem of style. With regard to vocabulary, what percentage of the books in Paul's library do we still possess? If the answer is anything like "We don't know," then a corollary to that answer is that we shouldn't be making any arguments on the basis of vocabulary usage.

Another answer to this objection of different vocabulary and style is a simple one. Different problems require different answers and hence different vocabulary should be expected. The same goes for style. The great Scottish theologian Samuel Rutherford wrote the tremendous book *Lex Rex*, along with his more devotional *Letters*. A close examination of the vocabulary and stylistic differences of the two books would be most interesting, and could prove things that would be even more interesting—albeit not very true.

In short, we should spend less of our time arguing with liberal scholars about the Pauline authorship of some of his letters, and more time giving a bit of grief to those evangelicals who think it is important to kowtow for some reason.

The apostle Paul is nearing the end of his life. In these epistles we find the kind of instruction that would naturally arise in such a circumstance—Paul is concerned with the next generation, and he is making sure the foundation is true and straight. Ephesus was the kind of place where this would be most important. The Church there was a significant Church in a significant place—Paul had ministered there for two years in the hall of Tyrannus. The ministry was very effective there. "And this continued by the space of two years; so that all they which dwelt in Asia heard the word of the Lord Jesus, both Jews and Greeks" (Acts 19:10).

It was no small work: "So mightily grew the word of God and prevailed" (Acts 19:20).

So many people were converted that the idol-makers felt constrained to counterattack—because "not alone at

Ephesus, but almost throughout all Asia, this Paul hath persuaded and turned away much people, saying that they be no gods, which are made with hands" (Acts 19:26).

Now all this was almost ten *years* before Paul commissioned Timothy to oversee the Churches there, which had to have been a real going concern during his ministry there. John wrote to the Church at Ephesus right around that same time—in fact, it is even possible that Timothy was the "angel" of the Church at Ephesus (Rev. 2:1). While the Church there had declined from their first love, it was still clearly a robust and orthodox Church (Rev. 2:6).

As we turn to the details of Paul's instructions, we face the challenge of our Churches becoming the same—both robust and orthodox, made more so by a return to our first love.

As you may have noticed, I will continue to use the Authorized Version as the primary translation for this commentary, but I've also relied upon the English Standard Version as a supplement.

1 TIMOTHY

SOUND DOCTRINE IN THE FIRST PLACE

Paul begins with his customary form of greeting, and then gets immediately down to business.

Paul, an apostle of Jesus Christ by the commandment of God our Saviour, and Lord Jesus Christ, which is our hope; Unto Timothy, my own son in the faith: Grace, mercy, and peace, from God our Father and Jesus Christ our Lord. As I besought thee to abide still at Ephesus, when I went into Macedonia, that thou mightest charge some that they teach no other doctrine, Neither give heed to fables and endless genealogies, which minister questions, rather than godly edifying which is in faith: so do. Now the end of the commandment is charity out of a pure heart, and of a good conscience, and of faith unfeigned: From which some having swerved have turned aside unto vain jangling; Desiring to be teachers of the law; understanding neither what they say, nor whereof they affirm.

But we know that the law is good, if a man use it lawfully; Knowing this, that the law is not made for a righteous man, but for the lawless and disobedient, for the ungodly and for sinners, for unholy and profane, for murderers of fathers and murderers of mothers, for manslayers, For whoremongers, for them that defile themselves with mankind, for menstealers, for liars, for perjured persons, and if there be any other thing that is contrary to sound doctrine; According to the glorious gospel of the blessed God, which was committed to my trust. (1 Tim. 1:1–11)

Timothy had been left with responsibility for the Ephesian Churches (v. 3). Although Paul is writing him a personal letter, it is also an official letter. Paul identifies himself here as an apostle of Jesus Christ (v. 1). His apostleship was commanded by God our Savior, and Jesus Christ is our hope (v. 1). The letter is addressed to Timothy, Paul's own son in the faith. Grace, mercy, and peace are declared as an introductory blessing (v. 2). The reason Paul left Timothy in Ephesus was so that he might charge certain individuals not to engage in "alternative-teaching" (v. 3). Such heterodoxy would include myths (esv), or what Paul in Titus calls Jewish fables (Titus 1:14), or other forms of cutting-edge scholarship. The endless genealogies are more likely of Jewish extraction than Gnostic, but commentators are divided. These disputes don't edify, Paul says (v. 4), much like disputes among the commentators.

The point of this requirement is three-fold: love from a pure heart, a sound conscience, and a non-hypocritical faith (v. 5). Some people don't like this kind of spiritual health, and so they turn aside into vain jangling (v. 6). They do this out of vain ambition—they want to be teachers of the law, and the only problem is that they don't know what they are talking about (v. 7). Other than that, things are fine. But, Paul says that we understand the law; it is good *if* it is used properly (v. 8). And one right use of the law is to restrain by force those who do not know or care to understand it (v. 9).

Paul then moves into a descriptive list of the kind of people who don't get it. First are the general descriptions: lawless, rebellious, those lacking piety, for sinners, for the unholy and profane. Paul then moves from the general demeanor of sin to specific sins. First we have father-strikers and mother-strikers (ESV), and murderers (v. 9). Then we have sexually immoral people, homosexuals, slave-traders, liars, perjurers, and anything else that is contrary to sound doctrine (v. 10). This right handling of the *law* is according to the glorious *gospel* of the blessed God, and the whole thing was committed to Paul's trust (v. 11).

The apostle has little use for self-appointed teachers of the law who do not understand what they are talking about. They are fools without a point, and their teaching is, in a fundamental way, *pointless*. Where does it go? Why should we know this? Where does it get us? In contrast, godly teaching does not "minister questions," but rather drives toward the goal, which is godly edification. To edify means to build up. There is a difference between a lump-in-the-throat kind of blessing, and edification. A preacher who plays the emotional violin can make you feel good for a time, but at the end, what do you have? Nothing. As the ancient rhetoricians would have put it, nothing dries more quickly than a tear. An edifying preacher or teacher gives you a brick, and, when you get home, you know exactly where in the wall to put it. As a result, the structure goes up.

As mentioned before, Paul addresses the *attitude* of rebellion first (v. 9). What kind of sinful tree produces the fruit of *sins*? The answer is a lawless, disobedient, ungodly, sinful, unholy, and profane heart. This is a certain attitude toward God and His law before there is any actual knowledge of the content of His law.

But then what kind of fruit grows on this tree? The first is those who strike father or mother. This is a violation of the first commandment with promise, and so it is also the first commandment with a curse. Then we have murderers. Remember this as you are studying your entertainment catechisms. The same thing is true of the sexually lax. The word translated *whoremonger* here is *pornois*, and it involves more than sin with prostitutes. It refers to general sexual uncleanness. Also contrary to sound doctrine is the sodomite. Also mentioned in 1 Cor. 6:9 is the effeminate catamite. So if words have meaning, the current push in the broader Church to allow for this kind of behavior is a sure mark of unfolding apostasy. Then come the slave-traders, liars, and perjurers. All this is contrary to sound doctrine, and there are a number of other *unmentioned* things that would be contrary to sound doctrine as well.

We should also consider the nature of sound doctrine. One of the striking things about this passage is that Paul does not divide everything up into neat, little parcels— with ethics *here*, and theology over *there*. The practical teaching about what was consistent with Christian profession is called *sound doctrine* and, even though a good deal of it had to do with developing a right attitude toward the *law*, Paul says that all his teaching on the subject was in accordance with the glorious *gospel*.

It is also important to note that doctrine for Paul was an ethical matter. It is common among evangelicals to insist that we need more than orthodoxy, right doctrine—we also need orthopraxy, right living. While we may sympathize with the desire to insist on both them, it should at least be remarked that for the apostle Paul, they were all the same thing.

MERCY AND GLORY

God advances His kingdom in the world, and because He calls fallen men to be His ministers, He is always working with flawed instruments. The only exception, of course, was the Lord Jesus Himself, but everyone else, from the apostles on down, has had to deal with their inadequacies for the task.

> And I thank Christ Jesus our Lord, who hath enabled me, for that he counted me faithful, putting me into the ministry; Who was before a blasphemer, and a persecutor, and injurious: but I obtained mercy, because I did it ignorantly in unbelief. And the grace of our Lord was exceeding abundant with faith and love which is

in Christ Jesus. This is a faithful saying, and worthy of all acceptation, that Christ Jesus came into the world to save sinners; of whom I am chief. Howbeit for this cause I obtained mercy, that in me first Jesus Christ might shew forth all longsuffering, for a pattern to them which should hereafter believe on him to life everlasting. Now unto the King eternal, immortal, invisible, the only wise God, be honour and glory for ever and ever. Amen. This charge I commit unto thee, son Timothy, according to the prophecies which went before on thee, that thou by them mightest war a good warfare; Holding faith, and a good conscience; which some having put away concerning faith have made shipwreck: Of whom is Hymenaeus and Alexander; whom I have delivered unto Satan, that they may learn not to blaspheme. (1 Tim. 1:12–20)

The apostle Paul begins with characteristic thanksgiving. Christ Jesus our Lord considered Paul trustworthy, and put him into ministry. The word here is literally *diaconate* (v. 12). Christ did this despite Paul's sins and failings—he was a blasphemer, a persecutor, and an overbearing and insolent man (v. 13 ESV). But Paul obtained mercy because he did what he did ignorantly and in unbelief. Despite Paul's great sin, the grace of the Lord was overwhelming with the gift of faith and love which is in Christ (v. 14). Paul then turns to a faithful or trustworthy saying, something that was current in the Churches of that time (v. 15). Christ Jesus came into the world to save sinners; of whom he was "chief" (v. 15). This is not true of Paul only, but he applies it readily to himself. The apostle to the Gentiles received mercy so that Jesus could show off with him—if God can save Paul, he can save anybody (v. 16). This results in a burst of doxological praise—honor and glory forever and ever are to be rendered to the King eternal, immortal, invisible, the only wise God (v. 17).

With this, Paul turns to the business of ministry. He charges Timothy to live up to the prophecies that had been made about him, and that he use them as encouragement in fighting the good fight (v. 18). He was to do this holding to the faith, and holding to a clean and clear conscience (v. 19). Not everybody does this—Hymenaeus and Alexander had made a shipwreck of their faith, and Paul had delivered them over to Satan (the realm outside the Church), in order to teach them not to blaspheme (v. 20). Paul is not being hard-hearted here. He has just confessed a moment before that *he* had been a blasphemer; he had hopes for the restoration of these two men as well.

A current movement in biblical studies is something commonly called the New Perspective on Paul. While many good things have come out of their work, and a number of the NPP advocates can be read with fun and profit, conservative believers still have to be careful. This is because one of the central ideas in the NPP is that first-century Judaism was a religion of grace, and that it was not legalistic or "Pharisaical" in the sense that this word has taken on. And this means that the conversion of Saul is seen as a "change of mind" about who Jesus was, and not a complete heart transformation.

The conversion of Saul is therefore seen as being more like Apollos being straightened out by Priscilla and Aquila, and not so much like a wino getting saved down at the Salvation Army soup kitchen.

The problems with this kind of theologizing are many, but this text presents an unanswerable challenge to this view. The unconverted Saul was plain old-fashioned *unconverted*. When describing himself, the apostle Paul does not hold back. He was the *foremost* of sinners (v. 15 ESV). The fact that all humbled Christians confess this together (it is a trustworthy saying) does not take away from the fact that Paul confessed it. And he is specific about his sins. He was a *blaspheming* persecutor and an *insolent* man. These are not trifles. Paul is not excusing himself in verse 13. So of course, first-century Judaism was a religion of grace—for those who had grace. It was a religion of legalism—for those who had no grace. Saul of Tarsus was among the latter. And this, incidentally, is why the question of authorship goes beyond a mere matter of labels. A significant point of theology rides upon it.

Respectable religionists always want to keep everyone in line with the "expected standard," and to appeal to the grace of God to clear up the little discrepancies that might show up from time to time. But God's grace goes all the way down to the foundations. Who did God pick to write the majority of His New Testament? A man who was breathing out threats and slaughter against the Church (Acts 9:1). Who was the chosen vessel to bring the message of grace to the Gentiles? An insolent man. And why? Because God wanted to sketch an outline of salvation (a pattern in v. 16) for anyone who would, in the manner of Paul, believe on the Lord to everlasting life. And that means that God saved Paul as an encouragement to both me and you.

We see that Timothy had his hands full. Paul brings Hymenaeus and Alexander into the conversation because they had some kind of relationship with Timothy—they were in Ephesus, or would be shortly, or Timothy knew them as fellow teachers (2 Tim. 2:16–18)—or something like that. Paul tells Timothy to live up to the prophecies that had been made about him. Notice here also that prophecy doesn't work like an automated conveyor belt. Timothy still had to *do* what had been prophesied that he would in fact do. Paul is telling Timothy not to shipwreck his faith in the same way that these two men had done, and this means that they were probably in a comparable position to Timothy's. This helps us understand the reasoning behind the qualification of the minister coming up in a few chapters.

All this is to be done in the presence of God, seeking His blessing. He is the one to whom honor and glory belong forever. Why? He is the King, He is eternal, He is immortal, and He is invisible. But this must be married to what this King has actually done in this passage. Glorious doxological passages like this, when we stand them off by themselves, give sinners like us the wrong impression entirely. We stand in awe all right, but we stand in awe of the Distant God. But what has the King eternal done, in this passage? He has put an insolent, blaspheming persecutor into the ministry. He showed *mercy* to a gnat-strangling Pharisee. He sent His Son into the world to save millions of really bad characters, all of whom could truthfully say that they were the chief of sinners. He picked a really hardshell case like Saul to show the strength of His patience. To use Augustine's example, God is like a doctor who moves to a new town, and undertakes (for free) the cure of someone for whom all hope has been abandoned.

Mercy without glory is compromise. Glory without mercy is despair. The two are brought together in the gospel, and *only* in the gospel.

ALL MEN TO BE SAVED

We now come to the practical instructions for the Church that Paul is delivering to Timothy. The point of the letter is to provide direction for public worship, and so here we are.

> I exhort therefore, that, first of all, supplications, prayers, intercessions, and giving of thanks, be made for all men; For kings, and for all that are in authority; that we may lead a quiet and peaceable life in all godliness and honesty. For this is good and acceptable in the sight of God our Saviour; Who will have all men to be saved, and to come unto the knowledge of the truth. For there is one God, and one mediator between God and men, the man Christ Jesus; Who gave himself a ransom for all, to be testified in due time. Whereunto I am ordained a preacher, and an apostle, (I speak the truth in Christ, and lie not;) a teacher of the Gentiles in faith and verity. (1 Timothy 2:1–7)

The apostle begins with an exhortation to prayer. We need to keep in mind that he is talking about prayer in public worship (v. 1). There are four kinds of prayer, but

they are all directed to one end—they are for all men, or
"all people" (ESV). What is meant by this? It is clear from
the context that Paul is talking about "all kinds of people,"
because he immediately begins talking about a particular
kind of them. We are to pray for kings and for those in authority, in order that we might live quiet, peaceful lives (v.
2). We should pray this way because God our Savior thinks
it is a good thing to do (v. 3), and He wants all men (all
kinds of men) to be saved and come to a knowledge of the
truth (v. 4). The reason he gives for the desire for all men
to be saved is that there is one God, and there is one mediator, the man Christ Jesus (v. 5). This Jesus gave Himself
as a ransom payment at the right time (v. 6), and Paul was
ordained to be a preacher and apostle for that gospel (v.
7). This gospel of truth was for all the nations of men.

When Paul begins addressing the liturgical needs that
Timothy would confront at Ephesus, he began by insist-
ing on a particular kind of public prayer. And from the requirement of this prayer, the nature of the prayer, and the
desired consequences of the prayer, we learn a great deal.

First, each local Church is required to intrude itself in the
affairs of the world. We are to pray for all men, from the kings
to the peasants, and we are to do so because God wants all
men to be saved. The Church is therefore a public institution.

Second, the Church is to accomplish this by means of
what it does in its public worship. This is the action of
God's congregated assembly, having assumed the center.

Third, we learn that the ideal circumstances for the
spread of the gospel are those of peace and security. We
are grateful that God's Spirit works powerfully in times

of persecution, and we are additionally grateful that the blood of the martyrs is the seed of the Church. But God says peaceful and quiet lives lived by Christians are the best means of bringing all men into the truth.

Fourth, we learn from this prayer what the essential duties of the civil magistrate are—the maintenance of public order and calm. The civil magistrate is the hall monitor of the school, not the principal. God is our Savior (v. 3), not Caesar. We must pray for the peace of Babylon, but we are not allowed to pray to the king of Babylon. We may desire and seek the stability of our American empire, but we must not be seduced by it. This is, unfortunately, a lesson that many conservative Christians have to learn.

But is this talking about all kinds of men, or every last man? Paul says here (v. 4) that God wants all men to be saved. What does this do to the Reformed understanding of election and the atonement? Well, it contradicts it if you take all men here in the same way that you would take "all triangles are three-sided figures." But if you render it according to a common usage in Greek, where *all* meant *all manner of*, the problem disappears, and that rendering fits better contextually with Paul's argument. When Jesus gave His disciples the authority to heal all diseases and every affliction (Matt. 10:1), this means that they had the authority to heal all kinds of diseases. God wants all kinds of men to be saved (v. 4), which can be clearly seen in this context. We are to pray for all (kinds of) men (v. 1), which can readily be seen in the itemization of one particular kind of man in v. 2—kings and those in authority. At the same time, we must not read this in a way that restricts the global sweep of God's redemptive design for the whole world (John 3:16–17).

The substitutionary nature of the atonement is also plainly declared here (v. 6). The word for ransom in Greek is *lutron,* and one of the words for "instead of" is *anti.* Paul combines them here into one word, *anti-lutron,* which could be rendered as "instead-of-ransom," or "substitute-ransom." He follows this up with another preposition (*huper*), which means *on behalf of*—His death on the cross is what He did as a substitute-ransom on behalf of *all.* Because there is one God (v. 5), and one mediator (v. 5), there is only one gospel (v. 6)—and there will be one humanity united in Christ at the culmination of all human history. Christ came to give His life as a ransom for *many* (Mk. 10:45).

Consider how the world is evangelized. Personal contact evangelism is not first; it is not the high priority. Note that Paul does not say that God wants all men to be saved, and that therefore, in the first place, we are to leave evangelistic tracts in laundromats. When you locate the root deep in the soil, this may not look like you are tending to the fruit, but that is exactly what you are doing. The first thing is getting the gospel right: Christ died on the cross as a ransom payment for all men. The second thing (and the first thing *we* do) is getting worship right. Note that Paul says that, first of all, public prayer should be made for kings and all those in authority, so that we will have public order and peace, so that we might bring the gospel to them. The third thing here is the public proclamation of the gospel— Paul was ordained to this task as a teacher, preacher, and apostle (v. 7). We do not have the office of apostle today, but we *do* have the first two.

Then, in the fourth place—not mentioned in this text—we may locate personal evangelism, according to a person's gifts and opportunities. *Do not let anyone tell you* that you are not evangelizing simply because you haven't explained the plan of salvation to a non-Christian today. Other forms of evangelism are certainly lawful (bumper stickers, billboards, tracts, movies, books, and so on), but the ordained means of evangelism is the liturgical public prayer of the Church for all men, coupled with prayer for the ordained preachers of the gospel. We have allowed our traditions of evangelism to crowd out the Word of God on this point. The question, "Did you share your faith this week?" should be countered with "Did your Church pray for the king last Sunday?"

THE GLORY OF MODESTY

We come now to a passage that has suffered much at the hands of expositors. I have no desire to take my turn at this, but the reason the passage has suffered is *not* because it is one of those parts of the apostle Paul's writing that is hard to understand. The passage has been greatly abused and twisted because it is *easy* to understand.

> I will therefore that men pray every where, lifting up holy hands, without wrath and doubting. In like manner also, that women adorn themselves in modest apparel, with shamefacedness and sobriety; not with broided hair, or gold, or pearls, or costly array; But (which becometh women professing godliness) with

good works. Let the woman learn in silence with all subjection. But I suffer not a woman to teach, nor to usurp authority over the man, but to be in silence. For Adam was first formed, then Eve. And Adam was not deceived, but the woman being deceived was in the transgression. Notwithstanding she shall be saved in childbearing, if they continue in faith and charity and holiness with sobriety. (1 Tim. 2:8–15)

In every place where God is worshipped, the instruction is for men to lift up undefiled hands in prayer. Two possible defilements are mentioned—anger and doubting (v. 8). Just as men approach God in a certain way, so the women are to do the same—but they are given some extra instructions. They are told to adorn themselves in a seemly way. They are to do so with a sense of decency (*aidos*) and good sense. They are not to deck themselves out like a circus horse (v. 9). Instead of ostentatious display, women are to dedicate themselves to good works (v. 10). The next command is that women are to be allowed to be learners, disciples, but they are to do so with a demeanor of submission (v. 11). The apostle then prohibits women from being teachers, or usurping authority over men in the Church (v. 12). The reasons follow: the first is the creation order (v. 13). The second is that the woman was deceived, while the man was not deceived (v. 14). Neither reason is grounded in the Greco–Roman cultural context. And last, she will be saved through the childbirth, if they continue in faith, love, and holiness with sobriety (v. 15).

We may begin with the holy hands lifted up. The Bible gives us many examples of different appropriate postures of prayer, and this is one of them. Standing, kneeling, prostrate, and hands extended are all commended to us. The key thing in this passage is that men pray in public worship with holy and undefiled hands. One defilement is wrath—irritation or anger at your fellow man. Another is doubt—wavering in your conviction that God is good and keeps His promises.

The original King James Version rendered the Greek word *aidos* as "shamefastness." This was mistakenly edited over the years to "shamefacedness," which is quite a different thing. Shamefacedness is the way you behave when you have done something wrong. The word *aidos* refers to someone with a robust and healthy sense of shame—one that *prevents* them from acting foolishly. It is not talking about how you act after you have been foolish; rather it is the sense of decency and propriety that prevents such foolish action. And when the question comes, "And why won't you do this with us?" the answer should be, "I am not shameless." So when women adorn themselves for public worship (and they are *told* here to adorn themselves for public worship), certain things should come immediately to mind. The first is that they are *adorning* themselves. The verb is *kosmeo*, and means "to set in order, arrange, make ready." We get the word cosmetics from it.

Secondly, they are not to be sexually provocative, and I would add as a corollary that they are not to play dumb when someone tries to talk to them about it. If you put a quarter in your pocket and everybody can tell if it is heads or tails, then your jeans are too tight. Third, women are urged to have a sense of shame, a sense of decency, of self-respect. Fourth, they are not to weave gems and gold droplets into their hair so that everyone at Church will stare at them. This is not "culturally conditioned." This kind of vulgar and ostentatious display would be as offensive today as it was then. And fifth, women who profess godliness should adorn themselves by being publicly useful, through fruitful good works.

Then comes the part that is so difficult for so many. Women are not to be ordained teachers. We want to be careful here. We must affirm what the Bible plainly teaches (cf. 1 Cor. 14:34–35). The form of the imperative indicates more than just a one-time event. Women are not to *be* teachers. Now the context here is public worship, and so this indicates that women are not to be ordained to the function of teaching *in the Church*. This is not the same as saying that men must never learn from women, which would be ludicrous. That would collide with what the Bible says elsewhere. Women are co-laborers with the apostle Paul in the work of the gospel (Rom. 16:1,6–7; Phil. 4:3). And Luke is clear in Acts 18:26—Priscilla helped her husband in straightening Apollos out in his doctrine. So women are excluded from two activities—ordained teaching and exercising of authority (ESV) over men.

The apostle appeals to the story of creation and fall as it is described in Genesis. He does *not* appeal to the prevailing customs of Ephesus. It is too often said that the ancient world could not stand too much liberation of the womenfolk, and so all this stuff in the New Testament is an accommodation. But it is not an accommodation at all—it is a challenge. This challenge is directed at our contemporary paganism, of the feminist variety. It is also directed at the ancient paganism of Ephesus—that city was a center of Diana worship (Artemis in Greek), and in that massive temple the priests *were all women*. The apostle Paul did not require Christian women to be shrinking violets so that they would blend in.

The last verse in this chapter is somewhat cryptic. Some take it as a relegation of women to the task of childbearing. But as lofty a calling as this is, the problem is in the verb Paul uses here. *Sozo* means to save. It can mean preserve or deliver, but here in the pastorals that would be an odd use. In addition, what are we to do with the godly women who have died in childbirth?

A better explanation here is to see how Paul is tying this to the Genesis account. The woman was deceived (1 Tim. 2:14). "The serpent deceived me" (Gen. 3:13 ESV). She will be saved through the childbirth (1 Tim. 2:15). "I will put enmity between your seed and *her seed*" (Gen. 3:15). And the upshot is that women are not saved through child-bearing; they are saved, just as the men are, through "*the* childbirth," the Messiah of God, born of a woman, born under the law. Paul makes it general again by shifting to the plural halfway through the verse—"if they continue in faith and charity and holiness with sobriety" (1 Tim 2:15b).

THE OFFICE OF A BISHOP

Given the nature of the Church, and the message we have been given, it is important for the leadership of the Church to evidence in their lives the fact that the gospel *works*. In Christ we are proclaiming a new way of "being human," and because this is true, we take all comers, all refugees from the old way of being human. However disreputable, we are to receive all refugees into the fellowship of the Church (Jas. 2:3). But if we do receive them and nothing ever changes, then it would be reasonable for our message to be rejected. Thus we reject all the apostles the world might want to send to us, but we receive all refugees. But in order to keep this from getting all confused, we should maintain high standards for the leadership of the Church. This means that we must keep a sharp distinction in our minds between the qualifications for *fellowship* and the qualifications for *leadership*.

> This is a true saying, if a man desire the office of a bishop, he desireth a good work. A bishop then must be blameless, the husband of one wife, vigilant, sober, of good behaviour, given to hospitality, apt to teach; Not given to wine, no striker, not greedy of filthy lucre; but patient, not a brawler, not covetous; One that ruleth well his own house, having his children in subjection with all gravity; (For if a man know not how to rule his own house, how shall he take care of the church of God?) Not a novice, lest being lifted up with pride he fall into the condemnation of the devil. Moreover he must have a good report of them which are without; lest he fall into reproach and the snare of the devil. (1 Tim. 3:1–7)

This is a true saying. It is a good thing to want to be a bishop, or overseer (ESV) (v. 1). It is noble work, a beautiful *work.* In order to do this good work, he must be a good man. Good work must be performed by good men, and the qualifications follow. Such a man is to be blameless, a one-woman-man, sober-minded, temperate and well-behaved, respectable, hospitable, and a capable teacher (v. 2). He is not to be long at his drink, and he must be gentle, not violent. He can't be a brawler or covetous (v. 3). He has to manage his own household well, with all dignity, keeping the children in submission (v. 4 ESV). The reason for this last qualification is then given—if a man can't handle the pressing duties of a father, then how will he manage with the Church (v. 5)? He can't be recently converted, otherwise he might become puffed up and fall the same way the devil did (v. 6). And last, he must have a good reputation with those outside the Church—in order that he not fall into reproach, into the snare of the devil (v. 7).

What is a bishop? The word is translated from the Greek word *episkopos,* from which we obviously get "episcopal." The first thing to note is that it is important for us to refrain from projecting two thousand years of subsequent history back onto the first-century use of the word. The word means "overseer," and it comes from Greek secular usage. A good equivalent would be something like "manager" or "foreman." In the New Testament it is used interchangeably with *presbyteros,* which comes from the Hebrew usage and means "elder."

These are two titles for the same office. Here are some examples. The apostle Paul sent for the *elders* of the Church at Ephesus (Acts 20:17), and in the course of his talk to them he said that they were all *bishops* (Acts 20:28). The apostle

Peter wrote to his "fellow *elders*," and he mentioned them "serving as *bishops*" (1 Pet. 5:1–2). The apostle Paul wrote to the Church at Philippi, and he addressed the congregation together with the "bishops and deacons" (Phil. 1:1). And last, in the book of Titus, Paul told Titus to appoint "elders." He then hastens to add that a *bishop* must be blameless (Titus 1:5–7). If words mean anything, the New Testament never applies the word *bishop* to a ruler over the regional Churches. *That* has to wait for Ignatius of Antioch (A.D. 110).

There are ten characteristics mentioned here that we might cluster under the first one mentioned, which is the general one of blamelessness. This does not mean "without sin," because, if it did, we would all be up a creek without a book of Church order. But the *blameless* overseer must be (or have):

1. *A one-woman man* (v. 2): the history of the Church has seen a great deal of debate over this one. Some have seen it as a requirement to marry, others hold that it excludes polygamists, others that it excludes those who have divorced and remarried, others that it excludes those who have been widowed and remarried, and others that it excludes those who are unfaithful to their marriage vows. The last is the most likely, although some of the others are picked up by this.

2. *Self-controlled* (v. 2): We can take four words together here. He must be sober and vigilant, he must be sensible, and he must be of good behavior. He is sensible and sober within, and dignified and respectable without.

3. *Hospitable* (v. 2): The word here literally means a "lover of strangers."

4. *A capable teacher* (v. 2): there are two possibilities here. One is that this word (*didaktikon*) means an apt teacher, and this is placed in a list of moral qualifications to contextualize it properly. The other option is a rarer definition of the word, which means "teachable."

5. *Sane drinking habits* (v. 3): he is not to be "alongside the wine." In the Old Testament, priests were forbidden to drink while on duty (Lev. 10:1ff). Drinking interfered with the prophetic office as well (Is. 28:7ff). This does *not* require him to be a teetotaler.

6. *A reasonable temperament* (v. 3): he will not be a bully, either with hand or tongue. He will not be violent, not quarrelsome (ESV). In contrast, he will be patient.

7. *A good attitude toward money* (v. 3): later in this letter, Paul says that the love of money is the root of all kinds of evil (6:10). Keep that particular evil off the session. False teachers were lovers of money (6:5; 2 Tim. 3:2). Micah prophesied against those who peddled the word of God for a fee (Micah 3:11). Also note how both Samuel and Paul considered this important (1 Sam. 12:1ff; Acts 20: 32ff; 1 Thess. 2:5ff).

8. *Household authority* (vv. 4–5): the man who would receive the natural respect of the Church household (v. 15) must first be seen to have the respect of his natural household (vv. 4–5). In Titus, we see that this includes the children being believers (Titus 1:6).

9. *Spiritually mature* (v. 6): the word here is *neophyte*, and probably refers to time as a Christian and not age proper. The danger that comes when promotion is rapid is that of conceit. The verb here is a striking one, and means to "be-smoke." Pride as a smudge pot in the heart ensures that the head will fill up with smoke. This happens more quickly if the head is empty.

10. *Good outside reputation* (v. 7): the outsiders are the non-believers. Paul obviously does not mean every last pagan (or he, *Paul*, would not be qualified), but he does mean that there is some value for us to be found in the "word on the street."

There is a balance between wooden perfectionism on the one hand, and a refusal to obey the plain teaching of these requirements on the other. The best way to proceed is to seek to establish a Christian culture in which all this is simply assumed, and when *reasonable* questions about qualifications arise, to have the elder in question either seek a sabbatical to get things in order, or to step down. The lives of those who lead the congregation are set forth as examples (Heb. 13:7, 17), and should therefore be *exemplary*.

DEACONS AND THE WOMEN

The apostle Paul then turns to the office of deacon, which is, in many ways, quite a mysterious office. We are given the qualifications for the office here, but an explicit job description is never given to us. We have some idea from the fact that the synagogue had a deacon, called a *chazan*, and from the election of "deacons" in Acts 6. But these are indirect at best.

> Likewise must the deacons be grave, not double-tongued, not given to much wine, not greedy of filthy lucre; Holding the mystery of the faith in a pure conscience. And let these also first be proved; then let them use the office of a deacon, being found blameless. Even so must their wives be grave, not slanderers, sober, faithful in all things. Let the deacons be the husbands of one wife, ruling their children and their own houses well. For they that have used the office of a deacon well purchase to themselves a good degree, and great boldness in the faith which is in Christ Jesus. (1 Tim. 3:8–13)

In the same way as the bishops, the deacons must be of a certain caliber. It is interesting to note that the early fathers Chrysostom, Theodore, Ambrosiaster, and Theodoret all say that Paul does not give qualifications for the office of presbyter here because the word *presbyter* and the word *bishop* referred to the same order.

Deacons hold a different office, and they are to be grave (v. 8), which is not to say gloomy. They cannot have a double-mouth, or be hard drinkers (v. 8). They must be upright with money (v. 8). They may be called upon to minister the Word in some fashion, so they must have a good grasp of the deep things of the faith with a pure conscience (v. 9). They should have a period of probation, and then they should serve as deacons (v. 10). The word "also" (*kai*) here may indicate that presbyters should be tested first as well.

The women have to be the same as the men—grave, with good control of the tongue, sober, and faithful in everything (v. 11). These qualifications run parallel to the first four things mentioned about their husbands, the deacons (v. 8). Paul then reverts to his discussion about the deacons. Each must be a one-woman man, just like the overseers, and he also has to rule his children and household effectively (v. 12). Those who discharge this office well are "standing on a good step" (v. 13), and gain the kind of assurance that comes from faithful service.

It is quite clear that the character required for the office of deacon is identical to that which is required of the elder. We have already noted that qualifications for *leadership* and for *fellowship* are different. But there are two things to remember in this regard. The first is that the leadership of the Church is not required to be this way so that everyone else won't have to be. They are to be examples for the congregation, not stand-in replacements for the congregation. And the second thing, which we will see in greater detail later in this epistle, is that simple repentance is enough to restore a man to fellowship. That is not the case with leadership—but it does not follow from this that a man cannot be restored to a position of leadership.

Following John Stott, I would like to point out the candidate for Church office (elder or deacon) must display a solid character in five main areas. First, in relation *to himself*, he must be mature and self-controlled in the areas of alcohol, money, temper, and tongue. With regard to his relation *to his family,* he must be faithful to his wife and an effective and loving leader of his kids. With regard to his relation *to others generally,* he must be hospitable and gentle. With regard to his relation *to outsiders,* he must be highly esteemed. And last, with regard to his relation *to the faith,* he must have a strong hold on it, and gifted in teaching it.

But what about the mysterious "wives" of verse 11? How did they get in here, and what are they doing? The Greek word (*gune*) in verse 11 can mean either as "wives" or as "women." Thus the decision about how to translate the word has to be made contextually. For moderns, the ambiguity in this verse causes interpreters to divide generally into two camps. The first believes that this passage sets forth the qualifications for deacons' wives. The second believes that it is referring to the women who are deacons. But there are other options, as we shall see.

It should be noted that the ancient Church had an order of deaconesses, as did Calvin's Geneva. But this represented *an entirely different office* from that of the deacon. This is crucial for us to understand, for various reasons. First, Paul has just finished telling us that women are not permitted to exercise authority over men in the Church (1 Tim. 2:12), and the office of deacon involves responsibility and authority. Second, the idea that women can hold the office of deacon was an idea that did not arise in the broader Church until the nineteenth century, as a compromise with the demands of feminism. Consequently, if we understand that more than one office is in view, the problems evaporate.

The deaconess was *not* a woman on the one deacon board. The office of deaconess was understood by the early Church to have been established in 1 Timothy 5:9–12, which we will consider in more detail when we get there. But for now, notice a few things:

> Let not a widow be taken into the number under three-score years old, having been the wife of one man. Well reported of for good works; if she have brought up children, if she have lodged strangers, if she have washed the saints' feet, if she have relieved the afflicted, if she have diligently followed every good work. But the younger widows refuse: for when they have begun to wax wanton against Christ, they will marry; Having damnation, because they have cast off their first faith. (1 Tim. 5:9–12)

There are *two kinds of widows* here—the kind that have lost a husband, and the kind who have been "taken into the number" and who have taken a vow of celibacy. The second kind are not recipients of the deacons' fund, but rather involved in helping to *administer* it.

Throughout the ancient Church, the office of deaconess was understood to have been established here in this passage. For example, the Council of Chalcedon (A.D. 451) reduced the age requirement from 60 to 40. If she married after being enrolled, she and her husband would be excommunicated. In A.D. 325, the Council of Nicea (Canon 19) numbered the deaconesses among the laity since they hadn't been ordained, but rather just "assumed the habit."

This helps us make sense of women in the Church who labored in the work with the men, as Phoebe did (Rom.

16:1). It also helps us understand passages such as this one in v. 11. And in studying the Scriptures closely we avoid both the heresy of feminism on the one hand, and the bluster of masculinism on the other.

THE BUTTRESS OF THE TRUTH

The apostle has been writing a very practical nuts and bolts approach to pastoral ministry, but we must remember that application and doctrine (in Scripture) are not locked away in different cupboards. They *always* go together, and in this passage we see how practical doctrine is, and how doctrinal our practice necessarily is.

> These things write I unto thee, hoping to come unto thee shortly: But if I tarry long, that thou mayest know how thou oughtest to behave thyself in the house of God, which is the church of the living God, the pillar and ground of the truth. And without controversy great is the mystery of godliness: God was manifest in the flesh, justified in the Spirit, seen of angels, preached unto the Gentiles, believed on in the world, received up into glory. (1 Tim. 3:14–16)

Paul is not telling Timothy things he has never heard before. He had spent a great deal of time with him in person. This letter is to support Timothy's authority in doing what he already knows he needs to do in case the arrival of the apostle Paul is delayed (v. 14–15a). *If* Paul is delayed, he wants Timothy to know how to behave in the house of God. Timothy almost certainly knows this, but it is important for Paul and Timothy to be seen as providing unified leadership. Paul says three things here about the Church. First, it is the house of God (v. 15). Second, it is the Church of the living God (v. 15). And third, the Church is the pillar and ground of the truth (v. 15).

Then Paul comes to a glorious poem/hymn. Without controversy the mystery of godliness is great (v. 16). Each of the six phrases begins with a verb, a verb which ends in the sound—*the*. Each verb is aorist and passive. Each phrase ends with a noun in the dative case, and all but one use the preposition *en* to tie the verb to the noun. I want to format the poem here to bring out some of the larger structure:

> Manifest in the flesh . . . justified in the Spirit
> Seen of angels . . . preached unto the Gentiles
> Believed on in the world . . . received up into glory

that is:

> Incarnation . . . miracles & Resurrection
> Seen by angels . . . seen by the nations
> Received by the world . . . received by heaven

So what is the Church? In verse 15, we have the Church described for us in three different ways. The first is that the Church is the House of God. The word *oikos* can either mean house (building) or household (those who live in it). We are both. Scripture says that we are the house of God in 1 Corinthians 3:16 and 1 Peter 2:5. And we are described as the family of God, the household of God, in places like Hebrews 3:5–6 and 1 Peter 4:17. Are we the building or are we the worshippers? Yes, that is quite correct.

Our God is the *living* God, and this makes us the Church of the living God. He, unlike the gods worshipped by idolaters, is the *living* God. Scripture describes Him this way in multiple places. Joshua tells the people that the living God is among them (Josh. 3:10; cf. Deut. 6:15). Even such an earthy detail as how the Israelite latrines were to be built was tied to the fact that God was the living God (Deut. 23:12ff; cf. Num. 35:34; 1 Kings 6:13). And faithful Jews were outraged when infidels made light of the living God (1 Sam. 17:26, 36; 2 Kings 19:4, 16). But God is not a subset within a larger category of "living things." He is life itself. We are in Him, and are therefore the Church of the living God.

The third thing that is said here is that the Church is the pillar and ground of the truth. This can be (and has been) distorted to mean that the truth is dependent upon whatever the Church might say. In other words, the truth is dependent upon the foundation of something else underneath it. But the word rendered as "ground" here is *hedraioma*, and *can* mean "foundation." But it would be better to translate it as "buttress" or "bulwark." The Church does not create the truth, the Church supports the truth. And the Church is also described as a pillar, lifting up the truth so that all might see and honor it.

True piety, true godliness, is a real mystery. So is lawlessness, by the way (2 Thess. 2:7). But notice the real mysterious nature of this real mystery. Godliness is *outside* of us. Where does *our* godliness begin? The answer is that it begins in the womb of a virgin. Why, when such things are preached, are the captives freed? Why do the lame walk? Why do the blind see?

Let us look at the three sets of phrases. The KJV has "God was manifested," while other translations have "who was manifested" or "he was manifested." It is Christ in either case, but the KJV has more clarity on this point of orthodoxy. This is a good place to note the unbelieving assumptions in much textual scholarship. When confronted with an "orthodox" reading and a "not as" orthodox reading, it is almost universally assumed that the orthodox scribes were industriously changing the text to make it fit. It is never assumed that heretics might do that. *God* was manifested in the flesh. We have seen Him, and believed it, John says (1 John 1:1–4). God was kind to the world, and proved who Jesus was (Rom. 1:4) by raising Him from the dead. This is how the Spirit vindicated, or justified, Jesus.

These stupendous facts—the Incarnation and the Resurrection—were set before the angels, and were set before the nations. This is our second set of phrases. And so what happened then?

We go to the third set. The world received Jesus, and the heavens received Jesus. Take note of the nature of public faith that the early Christians exhibited. This is the coronation march of a new emperor, enthroned on high. And so the faith of the early Church, pillar and buttress of the truth, is set over against two very common problems in the first-century world. The first is that this is the mystery of *godliness*, and not some mystery *cult*. Ephesus of that day was crammed with mystery religions, and this new gathering was not one of them.

We can see this in the second point of contrast. The fundamental collision was between this new emperor, Jesus, and the old gods—Zeus, Diana, Poseidon, and the like. The fundamental clash was between Jesus, the new emperor, and Caesar, the old emperor.

GUARDING AGAINST ERROR

Just as Adam was assigned the task of protecting and guarding his wife in the Garden, so the minister is assigned the task of guarding the congregation of God against error. There is always a need for it.

> Now the Spirit speaketh expressly, that in the latter times some shall depart from the faith, giving heed to seducing spirits, and doctrines of devils; Speaking lies in hypocrisy; having their conscience seared with a hot iron; Forbidding to marry, and commanding to abstain from meats, which God hath created to be received with thanksgiving of them which believe and know the truth. For every creature of God is good, and nothing to be refused, if it be received with thanksgiving: For it is sanctified by the word of God and prayer. If thou put the brethren in remembrance of these things, thou shalt be a good minister of Jesus Christ, nourished up in the words of faith and of good doctrine, whereunto thou hast attained. But refuse profane and old wives' fables, and exercise thyself rather unto godliness. For bodily exercise profiteth little: but godliness is profitable unto all things, having promise of the life that now is, and of that which is to come. This is a faithful saying and worthy of all acceptation. For therefore we both labour and suffer reproach, because we trust in

the living God, who is the Saviour of all men, specially of those that believe. These things command and
teach. Let no man despise thy youth; but be thou an
example of the believers, in word, in conversation, in
charity, in spirit, in faith, in purity.

Till I come, give attendance to reading, to exhortation, to doctrine. Neglect not the gift that is in thee,
which was given thee by prophecy, with the laying on
of the hands of the presbytery. Meditate upon these
things; give thyself wholly to them; that thy profiting
may appear to all. Take heed unto thyself, and unto
the doctrine; continue in them: for in doing this thou
shalt both save thyself, and them that hear thee. (1
Tim. 4:1–16)

The Spirit is very specific about this. He expressly *speaks*
what He speaks (v. 1). The phrase "latter times" does not
mean the very end of the world, but was fully applicable in
Timothy's day. It is most likely talking about the end of the
Judaic aeon (A.D. 70), but of course, applications of these
instructions would also continue down to the end of the
world, in any comparable situation. Some will apostatize,
falling for diabolical doctrines (v. 2). But they are hypo-
crites, knowing at some level that what they are saying is
false (v. 2). They ensnare others, forbidding the enjoyment
of things that God created as good (v. 3). Gratitude covers
everything (vv. 4–5). A good minister of Jesus Christ will
remind the people of this (v. 6). Paul says Timothy is to
reject fables and give himself to the spiritual disciplines (v.
7). Exercise profits a little, but godliness is the real deal (v.

8). The faithful saying in v. 9 is probably what we find in v. 8 and not in v. 10.

Why do we work so hard? The answer is because God is the Savior of all men, especially believers (v. 10). All of this should be commanded and taught (v. 11). Timothy should allow no one to despise his youth, but rather to set an example for them all (v. 12). In public ministry, Timothy should pay attention to three things: public Scripture reading, exhortation, and teaching (v.13). He is not to shrink back from exercising his gift (v. 14). He is to give himself to these things, so that his growth will be visible to others (v. 15). He is to take heed of himself and the doctrine so that both he and his hearers might be saved (v. 16).

So what kind of doctrine would a demon teach? The Holy Spirit is very specific in warning us against a certain kind of error. Ironically, this error seems very "spiritual" and religious, and *dedicated*. Resistance to this error seems very earthy—but such resistance is actually true spirituality. The warning was very much needed, because the Church has stumbled at this point *repeatedly*. Spirits do not just seduce into known error, but devils also teach falsehood (v. 1). The hypocrisy is found in the teachers influenced by these demons—they have a non-functioning conscience, one that has been cauterized with a hot iron (v. 2). What do they teach? First, they prohibit or disparage marriage. Sex is thought by them to be very unspiritual (v. 3). They are also killjoys in the kitchen, forbidding foods that God in His creational intent mandated for us to enjoy with thanksgiving (v. 3).

There is a deep prohibitionist streak in American Christianity on this point, and we need to know that we are particularly vulnerable to these demonic whispers. The Scriptures (objectively) and prayer (subjectively) sanctify all creaturely acts—from marital lovemaking to eating bacon the morning after. Godly Christians put refined sugar, the really white kind, into their coffee. And a good minister (*diakonos*, deacon), a good servant (ESV), is one who regularly reminds his people of these things. Prune-faced piety is not just something that somehow falls a little short. It is treason to the gospel. Food legalisms are the worst.

We can see the value of true godliness. Timothy is not to allow himself to get distracted by a bunch of myths and fables (v. 7). Godliness is something you work at. It is comparable to athletic training, which does a little bit of good (v. 8). But to be in spiritual shape is profitable across the board, in this life and in the next. What you do here matters eternally. We should take this to heart because it is a worthy saying (v. 9). This is why we work so hard, and this is why we endure such slanders (v.10). It is because we trust in the living God, who is the Savior of all men, and especially of believers. This use of "Savior" does not make Paul a universalist, or reduce salvation to a mere offer. Christ is King of the world objectively, and the lot of the whole world is completely different as a result. He is the Savior of the world, just as Caesar thought he was the savior of the people. But God is the *personal* Savior of believers. For therefore we both labor and suffer reproach, because we trust in the living God, who is the Savior of all men, especially of those that believe. This is what Timothy is to require and teach (v. 11).

In the context of leading the congregation, Paul gives Timothy a number of pointed instructions. First, despite his youth, he is to establish his example across the board, in every aspect of life (v. 12). Second, he is to build on the only authority a mortal man can have in this kind of vocation—that of Scripture. He is to make sure the Bible is publicly read, the people are exhorted, and true doctrine is faithfully taught (v. 13). Third, he must exercise his gifts (v. 14). Fourth, his private life must have public manifestations (v. 15). He must study what he is doing, and the people must see that he is learning, just as they are learning. Fifth, he must maintain personal and public balance (v. 16). And last (getting ahead of ourselves a bit and carrying over into the next chapter), he is to be prudent about all his relationships (5:1–2).

WIDOWS INDEED

The Christian faith does not encourage us to have romantic or sentimental views of human nature—as this passage amply demonstrates. But as we learn to live as God would have us live, we find that the results are often quite remarkable. The instructions here are primarily about women—and the expectations are, oddly, both low and high. And to what result? As Chrysostom once said, quoting a sophist teacher of his day: "Heavens," the man said, "what women there are among the Christians."

Rebuke not an elder, but intreat him as a father; and the younger men as brethren; The elder women as mothers; the younger as sisters, with all purity. Honour widows that are widows indeed. But if any widow have children or nephews, let them learn first to shew piety at home, and to requite their parents: for that is good and acceptable before God. Now she that is a widow indeed, and desolate, trusteth in God, and continueth in supplications and prayers night and day. But she that liveth in pleasure is dead while she liveth. And these things give in charge, that they may be blameless.

But if any provide not for his own, and specially for those of his own house, he hath denied the faith, and is worse than an infidel. Let not a widow be taken into the number under threescore years old, having been the wife of one man. Well reported of for good works; if she have brought up children, if she have lodged strangers, if she have washed the saints' feet, if she have relieved the afflicted, if she have diligently followed every good work. But the younger widows refuse: for when they have begun to wax wanton against Christ, they will marry; Having damnation, because they have cast off their first faith. And withal they learn to be idle, wandering about from house to house; and not only idle, but tattlers also and busybodies, speaking things which they ought not. I will therefore that the younger women marry, bear children, guide the house, give none occasion to the adversary to speak reproachfully. For some are already turned aside after Satan. If any man or woman that believeth have

widows, let them relieve them, and let not the church
be charged; that it may relieve them that are widows
indeed. (1 Tim. 5: 1–16)

The apostle concludes his exhortations to Timothy by
telling him what kind of relationship he should have with
the different kinds of people in the Church, and the two
dividing lines he uses were age and sex (vv. 1–2). Timothy
was to take particular care with the sisters (v. 2). Widows
who are genuinely alone and destitute must be helped (v.
3). But relatives have the first responsibility to help them,
not the Church (v. 4). A "widow indeed" is defined as desolate, believing in God, and dedicated to prayer (v. 5). This
is contrasted with a woman who lives in simple pleasure—
she is living in death (v. 6). The Church is to be taught
the standard (v. 7). If children or grandchildren don't take
care of their widows, they have fallen below the standard
of pagans (v. 8). Paul then makes it clear that to prevent a
certain sort of abuse, certain qualifications had to be met
by any widow who was enrolled to provide service for the
Church. She must be at least sixty, and has to have been
a faithful wife (v. 9). She must have a reputation for good
works—childrearing, hospitality, serving the saints, reliev-
ing the afflicted—in short, all kinds of good works (v. 10).

Younger widows may not be enrolled because their sexual desires might lead them away from Christ (v. 11). They
incur condemnation and blame because they left their former faith (v. 12). Supported by the Church, and without
lifetime habits of godliness, they slide into real trouble (v.
13). Younger widows should get married, have children,

and guide their homes (v.14). Paul speaks about this from experience (v. 15). The family should take care of widows first, so that the Church can honor those who are widows indeed (v. 16).

We don't come to this chapter cold. The Bible has a great deal to say about our responsibilities to widows, so let us begin there. Our God is the defender of widows (Ps. 68:5; cf. Deut. 10:18; Ps. 146:9; Prov. 15:25). God gets angry with those who take advantage of widows (Ex. 22:22ff). Magistrates who rip off widows will be judged (Deut. 27:19; 24:17). Farmers were to make allowance for them by leaving the gleanings (Deut. 14:28–29; 24:19ff; 26:12–13). And it is a regular complaint of the prophets that their nation abused widows instead of protecting them (Isa. 1:17, 23; Jer. 7:5ff; 22:3; Ezek. 22:7; Zech. 7:10; Mal. 3:5; Ps. 94:1ff). Pure and undefiled religion is measured in terms of its attitude toward the widow and orphan (Jas. 1:27). In short, getting this right is not a trivial matter.

But what is an "enrolled widow"? In our discussion of the "deaconnesses" of chapter three, we addressed this briefly. Here are the basic considerations. First, this class of widow was defined by her *service*, not by her need primarily. What she received was "honor" (v. 3); enrollment was based on her character, not on need (vv. 9–10); the age requirement meant that her need was not the criterion because need doesn't wait until sixty (v. 9); and simply getting off the deacons' list through marriage is not disloyalty to Christ (v. 11). These are clearly women who are "adopted" by the Church, and they are expected to have a proven lifestyle that shows that they would be a blessing to the Church. That arrangement, once made, was to be permanent.

Some of the early fathers thought that Paul was discouraging second marriages here, and exalting celibacy or virginity. It is just the opposite—he was *encouraging* second marriages here, and discouraging celibacy. This does not contradict 1 Corinthians 7:8, 40 because the women in view here clearly do not have the gift that Paul assumes in his teaching in Corinthians. And such enrollment was permitted only for women who were past menopause (v. 9) and who had no family who could take care of them (v. 16). This means that even if a woman was spiritually qualified to be enrolled as a widow, her family should *still* take care of her.

We learn some other important lessons in passing. Why should we take care of our own elderly family members? First, we need to *requite* them (v. 4). When they were in their prime, they did a great deal for us, far more than we know (2 Cor. 12:14). Second, we do this because it pleases God (v. 4). Third, we are to do this because it preaches the gospel, as opposed to denying the faith (v. 8). And fourth, we are to be concerned that the Church not be burdened (v. 16 ESV). Thinking ahead is important. We are to be diligent children, grandchildren, and relatives, not perfectionists. But don't kid yourself, and don't let "the system" buy you off cheap. Honoring your parents is a command with a promise.

What should these older widows *have* done, and what are the younger widows *to* do? The older women trusted in God and were given to prayer (v. 5). They were faithful to their husbands (v. 9). They had to have a good reputation for good works (v. 10), and those good works included bringing up children, showing hospitality, and being given to philanthropic work. For the younger women, Paul urges a second marriage (v. 14), the bearing of children (v. 14), becoming what he calls a "house-despot" (v. 14), giving outside slanderers nothing to say about us.

And in doing all this, what are these women *avoiding*? Obviously, they are avoiding the contrary of all the things already mentioned, but there are specific sins mentioned as well. Living in luxury is living in death (v. 6). They are avoiding rash vows (v. 11). Receiving a stipend from the Church without proven character is a real stumbling block. Women in that position would learn idleness, would begin gadding about, would begin to speak far too loosely, and would become fussers in the affairs of others (v. 13).

JUST AND FAIR

Justice and fair-mindedness can take various forms, but it always reveals the same kind of heart. Remember that this giving heart has already been displayed in the section we just finished, in the discussion of widows. God loves the *generous* heart.

> Let the elders that rule well be counted worthy of double honour, especially they who labour in the word and doctrine. For the scripture saith, thou shalt not muzzle the ox that treadeth out the corn. And, The labourer is worthy of his reward. Against an elder receive not an accusation, but before two or three witnesses. Them that sin rebuke before all, that others also may fear. I

charge thee before God, and the Lord Jesus Christ, and
the elect angels, that thou observe these things without preferring one before another, doing nothing by
partiality. Lay hands suddenly on no man, neither be
partaker of other men's sins: keep thyself pure. Drink
no longer water, but use a little wine for thy stomach's
sake and thine often infirmities. Some men's sins are
open beforehand, going before to judgment; and some
men they follow after. Likewise also the good works
of some are manifest beforehand; and they that are
otherwise cannot be hid. (1 Tim. 5:17–25)

Elders who rule well should receive double honor (v.
17). This is especially true of those who labor in the word
and doctrine. The reason for this is the teaching of Scripture in two places—the first being from Deuteronomy 25:4.
The second scriptural citation is from Luke 10:7 (cf. Matt.
10:10). Having paid the elders a just wage, other forms of
justice prove themselves equally necessary. Do not receive
accusations against an elder without two or three witnesses
(v. 19). This refers to the threshold of *indictment*, and not
simply conviction. But if this standard is met, and the charge
proves to be true, rebuke such an elder in the presence of
everyone, so that the others (presumably, the other elders)
would stand in fear. The apostle then charges Timothy to be
diligent in these things, showing absolutely no partiality (v.
21). One of the best ways to stay out of this kind of trouble
is to be slow to ordain elders in the first place (v. 22). Paul
tells Timothy to keep himself pure this way, and it apparently reminded him of Timothy's ascetic tendencies. So he tells

him to lighten up, do his stomach a favor, and starting drinking wine a little bit (v. 23). Returning to his earlier point, he says that some men's sins march into the courtroom ahead of them (v. 24). Others are not quite that way. The same goes for good works, and the principle stands fast—over the long haul, evil deeds and good deeds are seed in the ground and there *will* be a crop (v. 25).

The just heart is a generous heart. It is striking that we come from the section where Paul requires a right treatment of the widows, and then he moves to the Church's responsibility to be generous to its ministerial laborers. In that context, it is appropriate to talk about how to handle charges and trials. *Biblical justice is generous.* And so in this context, what does that generosity look like?

Elders who rule well are to receive double honor. This requirement has two elements—money and honor. The requirement is not fulfilled if a lot of money is given in a churlish spirit. Think of the double sense of our word *honorarium*. The first duty mentioned here is that of ruling well. This is not contrasted with elders who rule poorly (if they did *that*, then why are they elders?), but rather with elders who are good elders, but occupied with their daily vocation. Some elders give themselves to rule in the Church, and if this diligence of theirs takes away from their ability to provide for their family, the Church is to supply double honor. But some elders are more than rulers in the Church—they also labor in the word and doctrine. The Church is to make a special point of rendering this honor to them.

The reason for this is that the Scripture requires it in two places. First, the rule about oxen is applied to ministers in a "how much more" sort of way (Deut. 25:4). Secondly, Jesus said (Lk. 10:7) that a laborer should be paid for his work. Note that this shows Paul quoting Luke *as Scripture*. But the principle is equally clear in both testaments. When it comes to your enjoyment of the labor of others, don't be a skinflint. Paul addresses the same topic in 1 Corinthians 9:9–11. "For it is written in the law of Moses, thou shalt not muzzle the mouth of the ox that treadeth out the corn. Doth God take care for oxen? Or saith he it altogether for our sakes? For our sakes, no doubt, this is written: that he that ploweth should plow in hope; and that he that thresheth in hope should be partaker of his hope. If we have sown unto you spiritual things, is it a great thing if we shall reap your carnal things?"

A generosity of mind when it comes to ministerial pay needs to be matched by generosity of mind when it comes to processing ministerial accusations. This is because a minister who is doing his job will be working hard, and he needs to be paid. And a minister who is doing his job will also be getting into trouble. This is a sinful world, and it is minister's job to attack sin. When sin fights back, as it often does, it will do so in the forms of lies and slanders. John Calvin once said that "none are more exposed to slanders and insults than godly teachers." Because this is true, extreme care must be taken in receiving accusations against them. This is *not* because they cannot sin, but there must be a starting presumption that they have not. A charge must not even be entertained if there are not two or three witnesses (and anonymous blog sites don't count—Deut. 19).

"Ah," someone might say. "Where there's smoke, there's fire." *And,* they add under their breath, *we have a smoke machine right here.* It is actually true that smoke indicates a source, but we still don't know the nature of the fire. Is it licentiousness and self-indulgence? Or is it godly zeal that was making life uncomfortable for the envious and slanderous?

In this passage, we see how Timothy's growth in justice was to occur. First, he was to be appreciative and generous, teaching the Church to be the same. *Justice is generous* (vv. 17–18). Second, he is to be careful in receiving charges, but then impartial in administering the verdict. He is to play no favorites. *Justice is impartial* (vv. 19–21). Third, he is to display prudence and caution, protecting the Church by refusing to ordain pending disasters. It is easier to not do than to undo. *Justice is foresighted* (vv. 22–23). Fourth, he is to be patient, understanding that men's sins and virtues are different. *Justice is patient and discerning* (vv. 24–25).

Patience is important. Not every injustice is going to be fixed right this minute. Men sin differently. Some men's sins impudently head into the courtroom before everyone else—either because they think they are right, or because they don't know that room up ahead of them was the courtroom. Other men's sins have to catch up with them. The same goes for virtues. Some men's worth is evident at first glance. Other worthy men have to grow on you. But, taking the long view, we can afford to trust God.

FALSE TEACHERS AND CONTENTMENT

There is a huge difference between reformation and revolution. When we are confronted with great social evils, the revolutionary response is to attack the evils in such a way as to multiply the evils, and sorrows along with them. Reformation approaches the whole thing with a different heart and a different spirit.

> Let as many servants as are under the yoke count their own masters worthy of all honour, that the name of God and his doctrine be not blasphemed. And they that have believing masters, let them not despise them, because they are brethren; but rather do them service, because they are faithful and beloved, partakers of the benefit. These things teach and exhort. If any man teach otherwise, and consent not to wholesome words, even the words of our Lord Jesus Christ, and to the doctrine which is according to godliness; He is proud, knowing nothing, but doting about questions and strifes of words, whereof cometh envy, strife, railings, evil surmisings, Perverse disputings of men of corrupt minds, and destitute of the truth, supposing that gain is godliness: from such withdraw thyself. But godliness with contentment is great gain. For we brought nothing into this world, and it is certain we can carry nothing out. And having food and raiment let us be therewith content. But they that will be rich fall into temptation and a snare, and into many foolish and hurtful lusts, which drown men in destruction and perdition. For the love of money is the root of all evil: which while some coveted after, they have erred from the faith, and pierced themselves through with many sorrows. (1 Tim. 6: 1–10)

Paul teaches that slaves who are in bondage need to honor their own masters (v. 1). They need to do this in order that the name of God and His doctrine not be blasphemed (v. 1). *All right*, the response might be, *but what if the master is a Christian* (v. 2)? Paul's response recognizes that there would be a tendency for a believing slave to despise a believing master, but he should go 180 degrees from what his natural tendency might be. If anyone disagrees with this teaching, Paul says, and does not buy the *wholesomeness* of it, then certain things may be inferred about him (v. 3). He is a proud know-nothing, one who dotes on verbal wrangling (v. 4). The result of this kind of wrangling is envy, strife, railing, and imputation of evil motives (v. 4). This kind of guy gets into perverse disputes and thinks that godliness is a way to hit the jackpot (v. 5). But contentment is the best profit (v. 6). You can't take it with you (v. 7). If we have food and clothing, we should be content with that (v. 8). Those who want to get rich are falling into a trap, and the result of falling into that trap is destruction (v. 9). The love of money is a good way to destroy yourself (v. 10).

There are just two things to say about slavery here. The first is the obvious teaching of the New Testament. Whether a Christian were a slave or a slave master, that status did not affect his standing in the Church (Gal. 3:28). Slavery was as common in the Roman Empire as can be imagined—about a third of the population of Rome was in slavery, and there were about 50 million slaves in the Empire. The New Testament does not require Church leaders to bring slave owners under discipline for the simple fact of owning slaves. *But at the same time*, certain principles were insisted upon—principles that, if followed, would ensure the peaceful elimination of slavery over time. In the meantime, slaves were told to work honestly for their masters (Eph. 6:5–9; Col. 3:22–25; Philemon; 1 Pet. 2:18–20). This is the difference between revolution (violent bloodshed) and reformation (*koinonia*). The fact that the New Testament can attack *social* evils without making them automatic *personal* evils is a mark of its spiritual genius. But when revolution goes after such problems, it always needs a simple rule so that it knows which heads to chop off.

But why do some not get this? The apostle Paul turns from this instruction about slavery, and works gradually into this as the next issue. And it is notable that he pinpoints a certain kind of person who is incapable of comprehending what he is saying. What is that person like?

As we shall see, the root of all the problems here is *discontent*. Discontent with money, discontent with class or status, discontent with the pace at which troubles are improving. This is the heart of false teaching.

What Paul says about *koinonia* reformation is healthy—wholesome. But some don't consent to it (v. 3). A false teacher's empty head does not keep him from being full of himself (v. 4). His heart and tongue are all tangled up—he has questions and verbal clashes. These produce envy, quarrels, verbal hostility, and jumping to conclusions about the motives of others. These men have bent minds and hearts and so they produce bent disputes. They think that piety is supposed to be a means of personal advancement, particularly theirs (v. 5). Get away from such people, Paul says. This is a wonderful description of the rabid revolutionaries of the early nineteenth century, and it is a vivid picture of some of the people who are still advancing the cause of their radical politics.

When Paul turns to the subject of money, it may look as though the apostle is changing the subject, but he is not. The subject started with Christian slaves learning *contentment* in that condition. Paul then turned to the turbulent and *discontent* spirits who reject this kind of wholesome teaching. And this kind of discontent heart always assumes that money is the ticket out.

We will be considering the subject of wealth in more detail later in this chapter, but the foundation of all right thinking on this subject is contentment. Paul instructs the rich later; here he is instructing the discontented poor—those who *want* to be rich, and who are not now. Great profit is found in a combination of piety and contentment (v. 6).

"Contentment" by itself is mere Stoicism, and the word used here was a common Stoic word. But our contentment is in Christ; it is coupled with *godliness*, with piety. Like Job, we came into the world naked, and we will leave it the same way. Hearses aren't built with a trailer hitch for the U-Haul. Settle for, and be content with, food and covering (clothing and shelter) (v. 8).

Those who don't have wealth and who really want it are asking to be drowned in misery (v. 9). The pursuit of a *false* good will result in the obtaining of *real* evils. The love of money is a root of all kinds of evil. Note that you can love money without having any. Money is a canker that can consume the poor as well as the rich. When men covet this, it causes them to stray from the faith, and to impale themselves on the spikes of sorrow.

A GOOD CONFESSION

As we conclude our consideration of this epistle to Timothy, we will be reminded of the false teaching that would *rob* us of our inheritance, and of the riches of this world which would *distract* us away from it. And we will also be reminded, in a wonderful way, of just how glorious that inheritance actually is.

> But thou, O man of God, flee these things; and follow after righteousness, godliness, faith, love, patience, meekness. Fight the good fight of faith, lay hold on eternal life, whereunto thou art also called, and hast professed a good profession before many witnesses. I give thee charge in the sight of God, who quickeneth all things, and before Christ Jesus, who before Pontius Pilate witnessed a good confession; That thou keep this commandment without spot, unrebukable, until the appearing of our Lord Jesus Christ: Which in his times he shall shew, who is the blessed and only Potentate, the King of kings, and Lord of lords; Who only hath immortality, dwelling in the light which no man can approach unto; whom no man hath seen, nor can see: to whom be honour and power everlasting. Amen. Charge them that are rich in this world, that they be not highminded, nor trust in uncertain riches, but in the living God, who giveth us richly all things to enjoy; That they do good, that they be rich in good

works, ready to distribute, willing to communicate;
Laying up in store for themselves a good foundation
against the time to come, that they may lay hold on
eternal life. O Timothy, keep that which is committed
to thy trust, avoiding profane and vain babblings, and
oppositions of science falsely so called: Which some
professing have erred concerning the faith. Grace be
with thee. Amen. (1 Tim. 6: 11–21)

In typical Pauline fashion, the apostle tells Timothy to
flee from one thing and to pursue another (v. 11). He is
then told to fight the good fight, an intense athletic metaphor (v. 12). In doing this, he is imitating the Lord Jesus
who was faithful in front of Pilate (vv. 12–13). Paul charges
Timothy to make sure he does this same thing (v. 13), and
that he stand fast to the end (v. 14). The Lord Jesus will
appear in due time—and who He is will be revealed. He is
the only Potentate, the ultimate authority over all kings (v.
15). He alone is the immortal one, and He dwells in light
that cannot be approached (v. 16).

Those who are rich are told to avoid two things—arro-
gant vanity (v. 17) and trusting in that which is unstable
(v. 17). They are told to trust in the living God, remember-
ing that He gives us all things generously, so that we might
enjoy them (v. 17). Positively, the rich are told to do good,
to be rich in good deeds, ready to give, and ready to share
(v. 18). If they do this, they will be laying up treasure in
heaven, just as Jesus said (v. 19). Timothy is then told to
stay away from theological babblers and proto-gnostics (v.
20). Some people have professed these errors and have

wandered off (v. 21). And Paul then closes with a blessing and benediction (v. 21).

We naturally run from danger and chase after pleasures. Paul is telling Timothy (and us through him) that we are to run away from the desire to "get rich," which he has just finished telling us is actually the desire to get impaled on many sharp objects (v. 10). Timothy is reminded that failure to run from a desire to get rich is a failure that has discredited many ministries. You, *man of God*, run away from *these things* (v. 11). But in Paul's mind, turning *away* from one thing always means, necessarily, turning to something else. Turning away from sin (repentance) is turning to God (faith). Fleeing the snares of mammon *is the same thing* as pursuing godly virtues. They are just two aspects of the same motion. He is told to chase down and hold on to righteousness, godliness, faith, love, steadfastness, and gentleness (v. 11). This is *the same thing as* fleeing the discontent that would try to fix everything with money.

The apostle Paul was well acquainted with the athletic competitions of his day, and he valued it as one of his chief resources for metaphors of the Christian life (e.g., 1 Cor. 9:24–27; Phil. 3:12; 2 Tim. 4:7). He does that here in a really striking way. Fight the noble contest, your competition characterized by beauty of technique.

Paul then turns to challenge two idols. The apostle introduces us to the nature and attributes of God, as revealed in Christ, and he does so in a way calculated to offend two very powerful idols in his day—the first would be Roman political pragmatism, and the second sophisticated Greek philosophy. And he does this in the space of a couple of phrases. To say that Jesus was the blessed and only Sovereign, King of kings and Lord of lords, was a direct challenge to the presumptions of the Roman Empire (v. 15). And to say that God *alone* is immortal was a direct challenge to certain Greek assumptions about the spark of immortality within man (v. 16). Those who think that such challenges are somehow out of date are showing that they simply are not paying attention.

God is beyond all. There are four characteristics of God mentioned here. First, He is *invincible*, beyond the reach of all earthly rulers (v. 15). Second, He is *immortal*. We, at His pleasure, will live forever, but only He has life in Himself (v. 16). Third, God in His glory is *inaccessible*. His dwelling place is *inapproachable* light (v. 16). And last, He is *invisible*. No one has ever seen Him, and no one ever will. And here is the glory of the Father, whose wisdom is not like ours at all. God's own Word became a man. The invincible God was defeated and beaten. The immortal God was crucified and died. The God who cannot be approached took on flesh and approached us. And the God who is invisible was made visible to our eyes. As Jesus said, if you have seen Christ, you have seen the Father.

The previous section of wealth (vv. 6–10) addressed those who wanted to get rich. This section addresses those who already are. And in his teaching, the apostle wonderfully avoids the extremes of ostentatious display and ungrateful asceticism.

In the light of the things just said, those who are blessed with wealth in this present age should avoid two things (v. 17) and do two things. If they do, they will be rewarded with God's treasure (v. 19). They must avoid haughtiness and avoid trusting in their wealth. Their riches are to be matched by the riches of their good deeds. Instruct those who are rich in one way to be rich in another, Paul says. This is why they should be generous, overflowing, ready to share. The result is the inheritance of God.

Guilt is ungenerous. Gratitude is generous. Gratitude gives, and a guilty conscience doesn't. If wealth is a disease in itself, then why would you want to give it to others? But if it is good when held rightly, then by giving it rightly, you are sharing a real blessing. Augustine put it well—if you're the master of money, you can do good with it. If you're the slave of money, it can do evil with you.

2 TIMOTHY

GUARD THE DEPOSIT

Paul, an apostle of Jesus Christ by the will of God, according to the promise of life which is in Christ Jesus, (2 Tim. 1:1)

As the apostle Paul is drawing near the end of his life, his vocation and calling are still as clear to him as it became in the days after his transformation on the Damascus road. He is a commissioned apostle, one sent out, and the one who appeared to him and sent him was Christ Jesus. But Christ Jesus does not act autonomously now, any more than He did during the time of His earthly ministry. The sending of Paul by Christ was in fulfillment of the will of God. This in turn was a will that lined up with the promised life that is in Christ Jesus. In other words, throughout

the Old Testament Scriptures, God had repeatedly promised life to His people, and that life would come to them
through the Messiah, Christ Jesus. In fulfillment of that
promise, God determined that Jesus Christ should commission the persecutor Saul as an apostle, which is why
the Lord appeared to Saul of Tarsus on the road. All things
converge in Christ; He is the intersection of all God's pur-
poses and designs.

> To Timothy, my dearly beloved son: Grace, mercy, and
> peace, from God the Father and Christ Jesus our Lord.
> (2 Tim. 1:2)

The apostle Paul thought of Timothy as a true and dear
son, and addressed him that way. He had picked him up as a
ministerial assistant several decades before this, when Timothy was probably around sixteen years old. He begins with
a triune benediction—grace, mercy, and peace—and offers
this in the name of the Father and the Son. The Spirit is not
mentioned by name, but it is not as though He is excluded
from Paul's concerns. Someone once said that when doing
theology, you always have to say everything every time—
lest someone suspect you of heresy. But this is obviously not
possible; Paul only mentions grace, mercy and peace here,
but not faith, hope and love. What's the deal?

Not everything that is said has to be *said*. The Spirit is
the one who proceeds from the Father and the Son both,
and we see from our text that Paul pronounces a blessing on Timothy that comes from the Father and the Son—
Christ Jesus our Lord. The Spirit is here in the fruit He

brings, which in this case is identified as grace, mercy, and peace. The Holy Spirit is not mentioned as the source of the grace, mercy and peace because He *is* the grace, mercy and peace. And as this grace, mercy and peace, He proceeds from the Father and the Son.

> I thank God, whom I serve from my forefathers with pure conscience, that without ceasing I have remembrance of thee in my prayers night and day; Greatly desiring to see thee, being mindful of thy tears, that I may be filled with joy; When I call to remembrance the unfeigned faith that is in thee, which dwelt first in thy grandmother Lois, and thy mother Eunice; and I am persuaded that in thee also. (2 Tim. 1:3–5)

Paul begins by saying that he serves God with a clear conscience. He has said something similar in other situations as well (Acts 23:1; 24:16). His service of God in this particular instance is that of praying for Timothy constantly. Note that Paul's prayers for Timothy were a service rendered to God. Paul also says that he shared this clean conscience with his ancestors. This is striking, because in the next breath he points out that Timothy had godly ancestors as well—his mother and grandmother. This is all in the context of Paul's prayers, which is the desire to be reunited to Timothy—he remembered Timothy's tears and longed to be filled with the joy of reunion.

But there is another aspect to this. The pastoral letters are uniquely situated in the New Testament. They are much more focused on the next generation than other books.

Paul is nearing the end of his life, and as we piece together various hints in these letters, we see the institutionalization of the Church occurring. Paul has sought to plan for this time, and he wants faithful men to train faithful men, who in turn will be able to train faithful men (2 Tim. 2:2). That would take them well into the second century. It is remarkable that in a letter that is so concerned with the future, Paul begins with a testimony about the past. There is no way to be a helpful futurist without being a true conservative. Honoring the past in the right way is the best way to prepare for the future. Honoring ancestors the right way is the best way to become an honorable ancestor.

> Wherefore I put thee in remembrance that thou stir up the gift of God, which is in thee by the putting on of my hands. For God hath not given us the spirit of fear; but of power, and of love, and of a sound mind. (2 Tim. 1:6–7)

God both initiates and sustains. But the relation we have to what He does in both instances is quite different. When He first bestows on us, His action is unilateral, monergistic. But when He walks with us through the course of our Christian lives, He bestows and we respond. We work out our salvation with fear and trembling because God is at work in us to will and to do for His good pleasure. We work out what He works in. This is not what Paul cautioned the Galatians against, the error that thinks God does His part and then we do ours. Rather, God does His part unilaterally, and then God continues to work in us and that work is manifested in what we do. It is like Jesus raising Lazarus from the dead. First He spoke, and then Lazarus came alive. God then continued to give Lazarus the gift of life, which was expressed in what Lazarus did.

In Timothy's case, Paul reminds him that God had given him a gift, and that it was Timothy's responsibility to fan that gift into flame. The gifts of God are not to be taken for granted on the assumption that He will do everything. He *does* do everything, but He does so through us. Timothy had been given this particular gift through the imposition of Paul's hands. The reason Paul gave for fanning the gift back into flame was that God gave us a spirit of power and love and self-control, and not a spirit of fear. This indicates that Timothy was neglecting this gift because of some measure of timidity. The gift, whatever it was, had a tendency to get Timothy into trouble—as power, love and self-control frequently do.

> Be not thou therefore ashamed of the testimony of our Lord, nor of me his prisoner: but be thou partaker of the afflictions of the gospel according to the power of God; Who hath saved us, and called us with an holy calling, not according to our works, but according to his own purpose and grace, which was given us in Christ Jesus before the world began, But is now made manifest by the appearing of our Saviour Jesus Christ, who hath abolished death, and hath brought life and immortality to light through the gospel: Whereunto I am appointed a preacher, and an apostle, and a teacher of the Gentiles. (2 Tim. 1:8–11)

Paul begins with an exhortation to Timothy to not be ashamed of the testimony about the Lord. This tells us that there was at least an off chance that Timothy might be feeling pressure to be ashamed of it, and so we have to say a word about that. In the next section (v. 12), Paul says that he was not ashamed, but on various occasions in his ministry, he asked the believers to pray for him, that he would have boldness. This was not because Paul (or Timothy) struggled with stage fright. It was because the gospel presented a potent threat to principalities and powers who had every intention of fighting back. Paul had been flogged as many times as he had, for example, because he was doing something that threatened the establishment. That is the context of this kind of exhortation—don't be ashamed before tribunals and threats. Don't be ashamed before those who will try to flog you into shame. This can be seen in the phrase Paul adds—*nor of me his prisoner*. When one of the leaders of your new religious faith is in jail all the time, it might occur to some more respectable Christians that surely there must be a better way for us to frame our message. And by frame our message, they really mean *trim* our message.

Paul then moves into the testimony itself, that which is causing all the trouble. When Paul and Timothy suffer, it is not because they are difficult to get along with, but rather because they are "suffering for the gospel" (ESV). They are doing so by the power of God. Paul then goes into a description of that gospel, and we begin to see how antithetical that gospel is to the world's way of thinking. First, those affected by the gospel are saved and called to a holy calling. But though it is holy, it is not prideful—it is not because of our works. Our holiness is the result of His purpose and grace, not our purpose and work. This grace was poured out on us in Christ Jesus before the ages began, which takes us and our paltry works right out of consideration as a possible cause. That grace before creation is manifested now in the appearing of Jesus Christ, who abolished death in His resurrection, and brought life and immortality out to center stage through the gospel. Paul was appointed a preacher, apostle and teacher of all this, and the more he talked about it, the more the world's agents insisted on getting that message off center stage. Their method was to disgrace and dishonor the emissaries. But Paul knew that it is grace to be disgrace and an honor to be dishonored.

> For the which cause I also suffer these things: nevertheless I am not ashamed: for I know whom I have believed, and am persuaded that he is able to keep that which I have committed unto him against that day. Hold fast the form of sound words, which thou hast heard of me, in faith and love which is in Christ Jesus. That good thing which was committed unto thee keep by the Holy Ghost which dwelleth in us. (2 Tim. 1:12–14)

Paul suffers with intelligence, and he does not allow that suffering to function as an incentive to get him to feel ashamed. This attitude of his is what he is exhorting Timothy to aspire to. If everybody in the world left everyone else completely alone, there would never be any reason to be ashamed. But the world offers incentives to shame, and included in those incentives are sufferings (many of which are shameful, like prison). Who normally goes to prison?

But the reason Paul was not ashamed was that he knew the one in whom he had trusted. Trusting in Jesus Christ meant that he did not trust the assessment of the world. Paul had had the gospel entrusted to him, and he knew that Christ was guarding what Paul himself was guarding. After Paul died, Christ continued to guard it. But this does not mean that we can become careless about it—Paul did not have a fatalistic view of God's sovereignty. The fact that Christ was guarding what had been entrusted to Paul was not grounds for Paul to become negligent—quite the reverse. And Paul urges Timothy to take the same view. Because Christ is protecting the "pattern of sound words" (ESV), this means that Timothy should take care to follow those same words. But he is not to follow the pattern of sound words like a doctrine-monger—he is to do this in the faith and love that are found in Christ. Further, this pattern, this "good deposit" (ESV) has been entrusted to Timothy, and he is to guard it by the Holy Spirit who dwells within us as Christians. The gospel had been entrusted to Paul, who entrusted it to Timothy, and both were to labor in protecting that gospel as they knew God was protecting it as well.

> This thou knowest, that all they which are in Asia be turned away from me; of whom are Phygellus and Hermogenes. The Lord give mercy unto the house of Onesiphorus; for he oft refreshed me, and was not

ashamed of my chain: But, when he was in Rome, he
sought me out very diligently, and found me. The Lord
grant unto him that he may find mercy of the Lord
in that day: and in how many things he ministered
unto me at Ephesus, thou knowest very well. (2 Tim.
1: 15–18)

Paul is urging Timothy not to give way to a very natural temptation. When Paul says that *"all* they which are
in Asia" turned away from him, he is talking about all the
Christians in Asia. Paul was accused of being a master
troublemaker, and it would not do to be standing too close
to him. You might damage your testimony in the Christian
Church if you get too close to an *apostle* of the Christian
Church. Among those who had made this rudimentary mistake were Phygelus and Hermogenes. The irony is that by
trying to spare their names and reputations from shame,
the only thing we will know about them to the end of the
world will be their cowardice. On the flip side, we know
the courage of Onesiphorus, and his household. He was
not ashamed of Paul's chains—when he was in Rome, he
hunted Paul down so that he could be associated with him.
He was also faithful in his service to Paul in Ephesus. His
character was constant, even though locations changed.
Paul earnestly invokes the Lord's blessing on Onesiphorus
when the day finally comes when all motives are weighed.

    This was a problem in the first century, and it is a prob-
lem now. Christians are more concerned with respectabili-
ty than with righteousness. They are more concerned with
putting up a fine show for man, than with lifting up pure

hearts before God. Let a public controversy break out, and many Christians—"all they which are in Asia"—will head for the tall grass, and will blame the Christian who is standing in the arena facing the lions for being too provocative.

FINDING FAITHFUL MEN

> Thou therefore, my son, be strong in the grace that is in Christ Jesus. And the things that thou hast heard of me among many witnesses, the same commit thou to faithful men, who shall be able to teach others also. (2 Tim. 2:1–2)

Paul next tells Timothy to be strong against the fears that will assault any minister who intends to be faithful all the way down. Faithfulness leads to trouble, and great faithfulness leads to great trouble—calling for great courage. Having received that strengthening and equipping, Timothy is charged to train other men to do the same. What Paul had charged Timothy to do—in the presence of many witnesses—he was to pass on to others. Just as Paul had delivered this charge to the faithful man, Timothy, so Timothy was to find faithful men and do the same for them. They in turn were to receive this charge with the understanding that they were to do the same. We have four generations of ministers mentioned here—Paul to Timothy, Timothy to faithful men, and faithful men to the next generation of faithful men. Notice also the assumption that the training of ministers for the Church is to be undertaken by the Church. Instead of individuals "feeling the call" and paying for graduate school, we have the Church finding the men, and taking on their training.

> Thou therefore endure hardness, as a good soldier of Jesus Christ. No man that warreth entangleth himself with the affairs of this life; that he may please him who hath chosen him to be a soldier. And if a man also strive for masteries, yet is he not crowned, except he strive lawfully. The husbandman that laboureth must be first partaker of the fruits. Consider what I say; and the Lord give thee understanding in all things. (2 Tim. 2:3–7)

The fact that the Christian life is all grace all the time does not make it easy. Discipline is an essential part of it, and if we put this together, we should see that true discipline is yet another form that grace takes. The AV says "endure hardness" here, but the context is the discipline of certain kinds of callings or vocations. Three such callings are named—the military life, the athletic life, and the farming life. A good soldier does not get distracted by "civilian pursuits" (ESV) since his single focus is to please the one who enlisted him in the army. An athlete has to compete within the rules, and this means (incidentally) that he must train rigorously enough that competition within the rules is a possibility. And last, the farmer should expect to partake of the crops that he has raised. Paul says that Timothy should think about this, and the Lord will give him insight. It appears from this that Paul is saying something more in-depth than simply discipline is good for three callings, and therefore discipline is good for the Christian minister. Rather, he points to three different aspects of discipline, each one illustrated in that particular calling (although they all apply in all three). St. Paul says that a disciplined soldier does not get distracted. He says that a disciplined athlete competes within the rules. And he says that a disciplined farmer enjoys the fruit of his labor. Putting this all together—the disciplined Christian minister is focused as a good soldier is, he is rule-conscious as a good athlete is, and he enjoys the harvest as a good farmer does.

As an aside, it is important to note that Paul no more looks down his nose at the military life or athletic pursuits than he disparages farming.

> Remember that Jesus Christ of the seed of David was raised from the dead according to my gospel: Wherein I suffer trouble, as an evil doer, even unto bonds; but the word of God is not bound. (2 Tim. 2:8–9)

Paul's next exhortation is to remember the resurrection of Jesus the Christ. He did not come back from the dead in His capacity "as God," but rather as the offspring and seed of David. Of course Christ is fully God, as we confess, but it was Jesus in His humanity that died, and it was as the True Man that He was raised again to life. The resurrection is for humans. The preaching of the resurrection is essential to the gospel—without it we are all still in our sins. Paul identifies with this gospel, calling it "my gospel." Because he preaches the resurrection of the whole human race, as evidenced by the resurrection of its prototype, he gets into a lot of trouble. He is clear that he is suffering for the gospel, which is the gospel of the True Man raised from the dead. Because He was descended from David, He was a true man. Because He was raised to life forever, He is *the* True Man. The reason Paul is chained up like a criminal is because prisons and chains traffic in the old way of managing crowd control—they use death, and the threat of it. But Jesus told us not to fear the ones who could put the body to death.

The Word of God is not bound, and the Word of God centers on the message of the resurrection. Not only can prisons and chains not hold this message, or execute it, but we also see a hint of why prisons and chains keep trying to. Life forever cannot be threatened or constrained by the ways of death, but death *can* be threatened and destroyed by life forever. The message of the resurrection proclaims that the old way of "doing business" is doomed, and that the day is coming, and now is, when the dead will hear the gospel command to rise.

> Therefore I endure all things for the elect's sakes, that they may also obtain the salvation which is in Christ Jesus with eternal glory. It is a faithful saying: For if we be dead with him, we shall also live with him: If we suffer, we shall also reign with him: if we deny him, he also will deny us: If we believe not, yet he abideth faithful: he cannot deny himself. (2 Tim. 2:10–13)

Paul is a thorough-going predestinarian—all the elect are predestined to be conformed to the image of Jesus Christ (Rom. 8:29). But he is no fatalist. Note what he is willing to do for the sake of the elect. He endures everything, he says, for the sake of the elect, so that they might obtain . . . what? What Paul believes them to be predestined to obtain is the salvation that is in Jesus Christ, along with eternal glory. Lesser hearts than Paul's reason fallaciously in one of two ways. They either say that enduring *everything* matters, so anyone who shows the least sign of weakness cannot possibly be elect. Or they say that election is real and that it matters, and that it is therefore not necessary to endure anything. *Que sera sera.* But Paul knows that God ordains everything, including the means that He has ordained to accomplish His intended ends.

Paul knows that the ordained destination is reached by the ordained road. And if the destination is reigning with him, then that is reached by enduring. If the destination is living with Him, the road is dying with Him. The saying is trustworthy. The God who ordained the harvest also ordained the planting. The God who ordained the pregnancy also ordained the sexual union. The God who ordained that a man reaps what he sows also ordained that a man sows what he reaps. Predestination does not make Paul shrug his shoulders whatever. It makes him roll up his sleeves, and any other response betrays a misunderstanding of what God has revealed.

There is a flip side, with an interesting twist. If we *deny* Him, He will also deny us. But if we are faithless (merely), He remains faithful. To be faithless to struggling sinners would not be to deny *them*; it would be to deny Himself. He will never leave us or forsake us—despite our faithlessness.

A WORKER APPROVED

> Of these things put them in remembrance, charging
> them before the Lord that they strive not about words
> to no profit, but to the subverting of the hearers. (2
> Tim. 2:14)

Paul tells Timothy to remind his people of "these things."
What he is referring to is the set of truths just stated—if we
die with Christ, we will live with Him. If we suffer, we will
reign. If we deny Him, He will deny us. If we stagger in our
faith, He remains constant. Wise pastoral care reminds the
people of God that the way we live and speak now matters
forever. How can we get Him to deny us? By *denying* Him,
which is a sin of the tongue. In the charge that follows, we
cannot learn that words don't matter, because we have just
seen that they matter very much indeed.

Paul wants Timothy to tell his people, charging them not
to quarrel over words. This kind of thing is worthless. It does
no good, but only wrecks the hearers. There are a number of
important things here. Note that he says that this ruins the
hearers, not the participants (presumably, they are already
ruined). Those who listen to stupid quarrels over words are
torn down by the process. But those who engage in this kind
of thing think they are doing good, which is what Paul is
concerned to deny. This has "no profit," contrary to what
the disputant would say in defense of his logomachy. The
jouster with words wants to represent himself as "contending for the faith," which the apostles did, and which the heirs
of the apostles did. But for every Athanasius contending for
the truth (with words) we could find ten janglers in Church

history who contended for words with words. This usually led to a contending for more words, with more words.

Wise men see the referent through the window of the word. When they contend, they contend for the thing. Foolish men like the sound of their own voice, and additional words enable them to stretch out.

> Study to shew thyself approved unto God, a workman that needeth not to be ashamed, rightly dividing the word of truth. (2 Tim. 2:15)

In a fundamental sense, no sinner is approved by God unless he receives that approval in Jesus Christ. This is our justification. But it is not the case that God relates to us in our justification, and we are on our own with regard to sanctification. We grow in grace (by faith) throughout the course of our lives, and as we do, we are seeking to present ourselves to God in a way that He would approve. This applies to all Christians, and in this text, Paul is talking about the sanctification of the minister, the one who handles the Word. We are to come before God in a way that seeks His approval, knowing that we cannot seek that approval from Him unless we have already sought it from Him, and have already received it. On *that* foundation, we can seek to have a ministry that meets His approval.

The fact that we who have no need to be ashamed strive to be working means that it is possible to be a workman who *ought* to be ashamed of his ministry. When Paul speaks to this situation elsewhere, he describes some Christian ministers as building on the foundation of Christ with wood, hay, and stubble (1 Cor. 3:12). They will be saved, but their ministry will be consumed. Others build a ministry to last, one that will be purified and tested with divine fire, but will gloriously survive the divine fire. Not to put too fine a point on it, we are living in wood, hay, and stubble times.

It is striking that the absence of shame that is commended here is an absence of shame that comes from a right handling of the word of truth. God is not playing hide and seek with us in His Word. He reveals to His Church what He wants the Church to know, and reveals what He wants His ministers to preach. Those who do so faithfully are presenting themselves before God as Paul urges Timothy here.

> But shun profane and vain babblings: for they will increase unto more ungodliness. And their word will eat as doth a canker: of whom is Hymenaeus and Philetus; Who concerning the truth have erred, saying that the resurrection is past already; and overthrow the faith of some. Nevertheless the foundation of God standeth sure, having this seal, The Lord knoweth them that are his. And, let every one that nameth the name of Christ depart from iniquity. (2 Tim. 2:16–19)

There is a certain kind of doctrinal chatter and speculation that is simply vain and unprofitable. You can identify it by the kind of fruit it bears, just as the Lord taught us. We are to judge the teachers by the fruit (Matt. 7:15–16). Such teaching, such doctrine, leads to ungodliness, and a doctrinal cover for ungodliness is always going to find a ready audience. This is why empty and vain theology can spread so readily—it spreads like gangrene and requires (spiritually speaking) horse doses of antibiotics. Paul then gives us an example of two men who were into this kind of thing: Hymenaeus and Philetus were maintaining that the resurrection was already past, and they were unsettling some believers. A similar form of the same error has reappeared in recent years, known to some as hyper-preterism, and to others as pantelism. This is the idea that all the prophecies of the end (not just some of them) were fulfilled in the first century. Note that Paul categorizes this as being more important than an error in timing. The entire nature of the Christian faith is at stake. If there is no resurrection of the dead ahead of us, then there is no such thing as Christian orthodoxy. The Christian Church (ecumenically) has not settled on much when it comes to eschatology, but the one thing it *has* settled on is that hyper-preterism is wrong—"Jesus Christ shall come to judge the quick and the dead."

The other thing that can be taken from this passage is found in two citations, the first from the Old Testament, and the second an apparent proverb in circulation among the early Christians.

The quotation from the Old Testament is from the Greek translation of Numbers 16:5 (LXX), and there are two things we can derive from it. The first is what it *says*—God identifies His teachers. The second thing, which is quite striking, is the context of Numbers 16. That is the place where Moses is facing a challenge to his authority, in just the same way that the apostles had to face challenges to *theirs*. Korah, Dathan and Abiram all said to Moses, in effect, who do you think *you* are? They came with a bogus argument about the priesthood of all believers—the whole congregation is holy, they said. Therefore they should have a part in the leadership, which doesn't follow. Moses fell facedown (Num. 16:4), and then he said to Korah and his followers that the Lord knows whom He has appointed, and that He would make it obvious on the following morning. This the Lord did by having the earth open up and swallow Korah's band along with all that they owned. Paul is clearly warning Hymenaeus and Philetus. The Lord knows the apostles He has established.

He adds to this the proverb: Holiness is not measured or gained by challenging God's appointed leaders; holiness is measured by actually departing from iniquity.

> But in a great house there are not only vessels of gold and of silver, but also of wood and of earth; and some to honour, and some to dishonour. If a man therefore purge himself from these, he shall be a vessel unto honour, sanctified, and meet for the master's use, and prepared unto every good work. (2 Tim. 2:20–21)

The great house here is the Church, and the vessels involved are ministers. Faithful ministers are vessels of gold and silver, and the false teachers (in the Church) are the chamber pots and kitchen pails with potato parings in them. One vessel is on the mantelpiece and it belongs there. Another is in the mudroom. Every great house has receptacles for refuse. A man set aside and ordained for ministry ought to want to be an honorable vessel and not a dishonorable one. One way for a man to "purge himself" is to repent of false doctrine, as Hymenaeus and Philetus mentioned in the previous verses needed to do. Another way is for an orthodox minister to cleanse himself of the carping sin of envy. There were men in Paul's life who preached the true gospel, but they did it with malevolent motives, wanting to increase Paul's troubles (Phil. 1:15). The minister cleanses himself from that which is dishonorable, and this means that he becomes "meet for the master's use" (who is obviously the Lord), and he is ready for every good work. His holiness makes him useful. In recent years it has become popular to think that holiness in ministers is a kind of crippling disease, something that keeps them from being able to relate to the world with adequate coolness. But the phrase is "set apart as holy," not "set apart as cool."

> Flee also youthful lusts: but follow righteousness, faith, charity, peace, with them that call on the Lord out of a pure heart. But foolish and unlearned questions avoid, knowing that they do gender strifes. And the servant of the Lord must not strive; but be gentle unto all men, apt to teach, patient, In meekness instructing those that oppose themselves; if God peradventure will give them repentance to the acknowledging of the truth; And that they may recover themselves out of the snare of the devil, who are taken captive by him at his will. (2 Tim. 2: 22–26)

For the minister, the Christian life is both hunter and hunted. On the one hand he is to flee youthful passions and lusts (v. 22). It is important to note here that Paul is warning Timothy against certain sins associated with *youth*, and he is doing this several decades after he first met Timothy—which means that Timothy was probably a teenager when he first began traveling with Paul. It is several decades later, and he still must flee *youthful* passions. Those lusts pursue him like a predator pursues its prey. And yet, at the same time, it is not enough to simply run away. Joseph did not just flee Potiphar's wife, but also pursued the blessing of God upon his life, which he obtained. In this scenario, Paul tells Timothy to chase down righteousness, faith, love and peace, and to do so alongside everyone who calls on the Lord with a pure heart (v. 22). Here we see the minister straining toward holiness together with all the people of God. He not hired to be holy instead of them, but rather called to be holy along with them.

Paul also tells him to stay out of stupid wrangles. He does not mean to avoid all questions, but rather "foolish, ignorant controversies" (ESV). Paul himself was in many controversies, including some which his enemies could easily have represented as foolish and ignorant. No, Paul here is talking about controversies that really are stupid strife-generators (v. 23). Why disturb the peace of the Church at Antioch because you disapproved of the seating arrangements at the potluck? If the servant of the Lord must not be pugnacious, then he should stay out of controversies that stir up that kind of thing (v. 24). Instead of strife, the minister of God must be gentle to everyone, able to teach, and patient (v. 24). When teaching the ignorant, he must always remember that they don't know what they don't know. Some of them will be belligerent, and they are to be opposed in meekness (v. 25). And if you make the common mistake of confounding meekness with weakness, then you should consider something my father taught me—*if you think meekness is weakness, try being meek for a week.* Meekness is opposed to those who oppose in the prayer that God will do what only God can do, which is to grant the gift of repentance (v. 25). When God gives living repentance, it is the kind of repentance that results in acknowledging the truth. When they do this, they are recovered from the snare of the devil (v. 26), and it was gentleness and meekness that dismantles that trap.

THE LAST DAYS OF WHAT?

> This know also, that in the last days perilous times shall come. For men shall be lovers of their own selves, covetous, boasters, proud, blasphemers, disobedient to parents, unthankful, unholy, Without natural affection, trucebreakers, false accusers, incontinent, fierce, despisers of those that are good, Traitors, heady, high-minded, lovers of pleasures more than lovers of God; Having a form of godliness, but denying the power thereof: from such turn away. (2 Tim. 3: 1–5)

Timothy is told that in the "last days" perils would come, and he explains the type of person who would bring those perils. The first thing to note is that Paul had in mind the last days of the Judaic aeon, and not the last days of the world, or the space/time continuum. This can be seen contextually in that Paul says that a certain kind of person will be manifested in the last days, and he concludes the exhortation by telling Timothy to turn away from those people. We can see this as the first application without reducing in any way the need for us to make similar applications in similar circumstances.

What sort of people would show up in the last days? Paul runs through a laundry list of sinful characteristics, and holds his surprise for the end. People, he says, will be lovers of self, which indicates that there is possibly a problem with our culture's insistence that everybody learn how to love themselves. They will be greedy, lovers of money (ESV). Their demeanor will be an insolent one—boasting, prideful, blaspheming. They fail in the most fundamental relationship—they disobey their parents. Their attitude is unthankful, and they do not care for holy things. Their hearts are filled with cruelty—they are pitiless, implacable, scurrilous, fierce, and traitorous. They have no self-control; what they want, they want right now. They despise the good, they are reckless, and they are swollen with vanities. Instead of loving God, they love pleasure. And now the surprise. From the description, we would be justified in thinking that Paul was describing particularly sullen members of some particularly tough street gangs. But no . . .

These people are in the Church. They have the form of godliness, but deny the power of it. Timothy is told to stay away from them, meaning that they most likely aspire to some sort of teaching or leadership office. Now if this kind of person has the appearance of godliness, it is plain that in order to pull this off, some people have to be looking at the wrong set of standards entirely. The power of godliness lies in avoiding the list of sins that just went before. It does not consist of pounding a pulpit, writing a thick academic tome, wearing a robe, praying through the nose in sonorous tones, or giving a big chunk of change for the new annex on the Church building.

> For of this sort are they which creep into houses, and lead captive silly women laden with sins, led away with divers lusts, Ever learning, and never able to come to the knowledge of the truth. Now as Jannes and Jambres withstood Moses, so do these also resist the truth: men of corrupt minds, reprobate concerning the faith. But they shall proceed no further: for their folly shall be manifest unto all men, as theirs also was. (2 Tim. 3:6–9)

These false teachers prey upon a certain kind of person, characterized here by Paul as weak women, burdened down by guilt and led by their lusts (v. 6). Just as the serpent in the Garden crept into the first family, through Adam's negligence, so also false ones creep into households in order to lead off the weak members of that household. The two things mentioned here that make a person vulnerable and easily led this way are the characteristics of being sin-laden, and of being passion-driven. The person involved is "ever learning," but never coming to closure (v. 7). She pushes the seat buckle and clip together over and over and over again, but she never hears the click. Paul then mentions two of the men (by name) who had opposed Moses at the court of Pharaoh, which perhaps gives us some insight into the kind of control that they had over Pharaoh. Moses comes as the one who will liberate, and so they oppose him—enemies of freedom as they are. In the same way, false teachers in the "last days" that Timothy will have to live through will oppose what he says, since his gospel would be the liberation of those enslaved by lies and deceptions. Such teachers have a corrupt mind, and are rejected as far as the faith is concerned (v. 8). At the same time, this kind of folly is a sprinter, not a marathon runner. Their folly will be manifest to all soon enough (v. 9).

And so we see that flitting from one intellectual fad to another is not an intellectual problem. It is a moral problem. Men of corrupt mind encourage it, and people who are guilt-laden and passion-driven fall for it. And after many years of this, they have to say, with U2, that they "still haven't found what they're looking for."

THE BREATH OF GOD

> But thou hast fully known my doctrine, manner of life, purpose, faith, longsuffering, charity, patience, Persecutions, afflictions, which came unto me at Antioch, at Iconium, at Lystra; what persecutions I endured: but out of them all the Lord delivered me. Yea, and all that will live godly in Christ Jesus shall suffer persecution. (2 Tim. 3:10–12)

Timothy was a good disciple, a good follower. The first thing that Paul mentions here was the fact that Timothy was a good student; he followed Paul's doctrine. And that is where we tend to stop, thinking that Christian discipleship is a cerebral matter—thinking in line with a doctrinal teaching or tradition. But notice that Timothy was a good disciple because he was a good imitator. Paul mentions doctrine first, but it is first in a long line of other things, all of which were character traits. Timothy had "fully known" (KJV) or "followed" (ESV), meaning he *imitated*, Paul's conduct, his aim in life, his faith, his patience, his love, his steadfastness, his persecutions and sufferings. The Lord Jesus says that the student becomes like his teacher, and this is why the character of the teacher is so important (Luke 6:40). This is why the professionalization of the ministry has been such a bad thing. Paul had suffered greatly at Antioch, Iconium, and Lystra, which were located in the region where Timothy was from. The Lord had delivered Paul from all of them, and so of course Timothy had been a witness of that as well.

Then Paul gives a general principle—all who desire to live a godly life in Christ Jesus will draw the ire of the world. They *will* be persecuted. Now we must be careful here in two ways. First, we must be careful not to commit the fallacy that is called affirming the consequent. All cows have four legs, but having four legs doesn't make something a cow. All who desire to live in godly way will be persecuted, but not all who are persecuted are godly. Some people are persecuted because they are obnoxious, although they like to think it is because they are holy. But when they make this claim they are making the same mistake as one who would try to get dairy products from a cat. The second mistake is to soften what Paul actually claims here. It would be nice if only one faithful Christian in a thousand wound up in trouble, but that is not what Paul says. Even if we take it as a generalization and not a universal claim, it is still hard to reconcile with our deep-seated desire for peace, security and comfort.

> But evil men and seducers shall wax worse and worse, deceiving, and being deceived. But continue thou in the things which thou hast learned and hast been assured of, knowing of whom thou hast learned them; And that from a child thou hast known the holy scriptures, which are able to make thee wise unto salvation through faith which is in Christ Jesus. (2 Tim. 3:13–15)

Paul has just finished saying that those who desire to live a godly life will draw the ire of those who do not share that desire. He goes on to say that evil men and charlatans are in a downward spiral, getting worse and worse. The process by which this happens is the process of lying and being lied to. Ungodliness, like godliness, is organic and grows. The moral condition of man is not static. On that basis, Paul urges Timothy to continue in what he has learned and believed. Both godliness and ungodliness are resources that compound with interest. We grow up into salvation, or we grow down into damnation. Timothy is reminded that he was given a good start, and that he had known the Scriptures from childhood, the sacred writings that are able to make him wise in the matters concerning salvation. But this "head start" is not treated as a supplement to faith—salvation is still through faith alone in Christ Jesus alone. The issue is that the human heart is so averse to grace, and so prone to develop workarounds to grace (some of them in the *name* of grace) that it is always wise to begin instructing children in the ways of grace early.

> All scripture is given by inspiration of God, and is prof-
> itable for doctrine, for reproof, for correction, for in-
> struction in righteousness: That the man of God may
> be perfect, thoroughly furnished unto all good works.
> (2 Tim. 3:16–17)

This is a description of a minister's tool chest. The "man of God" here is not a generic Christian, but rather a man called of God. Throughout the Old Testament, the man of God was the prophet; in the New, he is the man who has assumed the prophet's mantle. He does not give fresh revelation him-self, but rather is the man who has the compilation of that completed revelation in his hands. While he is not a prophet himself, he is the heir of the prophets. In other words, he is not limited by the cessation of the prophetic gift because, as it says here, he is competent for all good works. There is no task the minister will be called upon to perform that he is not equipped to perform through the Scriptures.

All Scripture is the breath of God, the exhalation of God. Because of what it is, the minister is fitted out for various tasks. In the first place, he has something to teach. And when he runs out of things to say, as my father taught me, he should go on to the next verse. Second, the Scrip-tures give him the authority to reprove someone as neces-sary. Third, he is equipped to correct. Reproof says, "No, not that way." Correction says, "Go this way instead."

And last, the Scriptures enable a man to instruct others in righteousness.

The man of God should always remember that Scripture enables him to do these things because of what Scripture is. If Scripture were not the exhalation of God, or if a minister comes to believe that it is not, then we are looking at a minister who has no commission, no real authority to teach, reprove, correct, or train. A man with an open Bible before him in the pulpit is a man who represents the God who is not silent. A man with a closed Bible is as much in the dark as anybody.

PREACHING THE BREATH OF GOD

> I charge thee therefore before God, and the Lord Jesus Christ, who shall judge the quick and the dead at his appearing and his kingdom; Preach the word; be instant in season, out of season; reprove, rebuke, exhort with all long suffering and doctrine. For the time will come when they will not endure sound doctrine; but after their own lusts shall they heap to themselves teachers, having itching ears; And they shall turn away their ears from the truth, and shall be turned unto fables. But watch thou in all things, endure afflictions, do the work of an evangelist, make full proof of thy ministry. (2 Tim. 4:1–5)

At the end of chapter 3, Timothy is fitted out with his armor. Here he is told what to do with it; he is told how to fight. Paul solemnly charges him with his task, in the presence of God and Christ—the Christ who will judge the living and the dead at His appearing and the manifestation of His kingdom. And what is that task? He is to preach the Word. Timothy was given the Scriptures to equip him in the previous passage, and so here he is charged to use his equipment. He has the Scriptures and he must preach the Scriptures. He must do this when people want to hear it (in season) and when they would rather not (out of season). He is to use the Word to reprove, rebuke, and exhort. He is to do this all while patiently teaching doctrine. Timothy is told to do this while expecting an unseasonable time to come—the time will come when people won't put up with sound teaching. They will rather prefer to have doctrine tailored to their passions than to have to tailor their passions in accordance with the doctrine. And if you need that kind of tailoring, then you need specialty tailors—those who will cut, snip and trim to order. Some people believe the congregation is in charge of the content of the sermons, but they are not. Some believe the preacher is in charge of it, but that is also false. The ordained minister is a minister, and he is charged to preach something that would have been true whether or not he or every last big tither in the Church agreed with it or not. The reason men veer away from the truth and wander off into myths is that they want a doctrinal system that leaves room for their lusts. But the faithful minister has none of it—he is to watch in all things and be prepared to catch flak. He does the work of an evangelist, not the work of a recruiter. He fulfills his ministry, and a delegated ministry it is.

> For I am now ready to be offered, and the time of my
> departure is at hand. I have fought a good fight, I have
> finished my course, I have kept the faith: Henceforth
> there is laid up for me a crown of righteousness, which
> the Lord, the righteous judge, shall give me at that
> day: and not to me only, but unto all them also that
> love his appearing. (2 Tim. 4: 6–8)

Paul is nearing the end of his Christian pilgrimage, and he speaks of his life as a believer and minister as a drink offering, about to be poured out before the Lord. A drink offering, poured out on the ground, looks as though it is gone forever, but God keeps track of everything that goes into the soil. Paul is ready to be done, and he talks about his readiness with a series of metaphors. The first is taken from the sacrificial system of the Old Testament, and he then follows it up with two athletic metaphors—or perhaps a military metaphor and an athletic metaphor. He has fought as a warrior or as a boxer ought to fight. He has run as an athlete ought to run, with his eye on the finish line. These metaphors point to the reality that Paul is describing. He has kept the faith, he has not wandered off or veered from the path.

Paul knows that salvation is by grace, and he knows that it is all of grace. He knows that the righteousness of Jesus Christ is imputed to those who have faith in Him. This does not alter in the slightest his willingness to speak about the awards ceremony at the end of the race. Paul's vision of the Christian life is the kind of event that is followed by the raising of flags, the playing of anthems, and the placement of gold medals around the neck. In his day, that prize was a crown, and he describes what he will receive as a "crown of righteousness." The Lord, who is Himself righteousness, will award Paul a crown of righteousness on the last Day. Not only will the Lord do this for Paul, He will also do for everyone who has loved His appearing. Those who love His appearing look forward to it. In that Day, the Lord will honor His gifts with yet more gifts. He who gives all righteousness will reward us for having that righteousness, and He will do it by giving us a crown of righteousness. It is the crowning gift that crowns all gifts.

FINAL INSTRUCTIONS

> Do thy diligence to come shortly unto me: For Demas hath forsaken me, having loved this present world, and is departed unto Thessalonica; Crescens to Galatia, Titus unto Dalmatia. Only Luke is with me. Take Mark, and bring him with thee: for he is profitable to me for the ministry. And Tychicus have I sent to Ephesus. The cloak that I left at Troas with Carpus, when thou comest, bring with thee, and the books, but especially the parchments. (2 Tim. 4:9–13)

Paul was an apostle who depended upon his companions—even when his companions weren't that dependable. Circumstances have conspired such that Paul was isolated, and needed to ask Timothy to come to him right away. He was left alone, with the exception of Luke, and he needed reinforcements. He asked Timothy to come to him asap. Demas had left, and not in a good way. Paul notes here that he left him to go to Thessalonica. We don't know what the occasion was, but we do know that Demas was motivated in some way by the wrong kind of worldly love. Crescens went to Galatia, and Titus to Dalmatia, and both presumably because ministry called them there. Paul wanted Timothy to come, and he wanted him to make sure to take Mark, who was useful to Paul in his ministry. This is the same Mark who wrote the second gospel, and who had accompanied Paul on his first missionary journey (Acts 13:5). Mark had left them, returning to Jerusalem (13:13), right after Paul had preached the gospel to a Gentile outside the context of the synagogue, for the first time (13: 7, 12). John Mark, apparently of the Judaizing faction, couldn't handle this and returned to Jerusalem. If he was the rich, young ruler (the gospel of Mark is the only one that records how Jesus loved him), we can piece some of this together. He was wealthy, an inhabitant of Jerusalem, and devoted to the law. He left Paul over the Gentile issue, but after the Jerusalem council made its determination, he submitted to that decision. This is why Barnabas was willing to take him on the next journey (Acts 15:37), and yet we can see why Paul was unwilling to do so (Acts 15:38). Barnabas was a true son of encouragement, and Paul had profound reasons for being suspicious of every form of Judaizing. But here, near the end of Paul's life, we see Paul's acknowledgment that Barnabas had been right, if not in his judgment about that particular missionary journey, at least right in his assessment of Mark's character.

It is quite striking that in this place Paul marks how he had been deserted by someone who was in love with the present world, Demas, and he remarks on how useful someone else was, Mark, a man who had once deserted him in much the same way that Demas had.

> Alexander the coppersmith did me much evil: the Lord reward him according to his works: Of whom be thou ware also; for he hath greatly withstood our words. At my first answer no man stood with me, but all men forsook me: I pray God that it may not be laid to their charge. Notwithstanding the Lord stood with me, and strengthened me; that by me the preaching might be fully known, and that all the Gentiles might hear: and I was delivered out of the mouth of the lion. And the Lord shall deliver me from every evil work, and will preserve me unto his heavenly kingdom: to whom be glory for ever and ever. Amen. (2 Tim. 4:14–18)

We don't know who this Alexander was, but we know that he was a coppersmith and that he strongly opposed the message Paul was preaching. This, and the fact that Paul calls down an imprecation, would seem to indicate that he was opposing the gospel from outside the faith, instead of being a false teacher within the confines of the Church. Perhaps he was someone whose business was affected by the gospel, as happened in Ephesus with Demetrius the silversmith (Acts 19:24). Notice that Paul calls for strict justice in his case, for him to be repaid according to his works (v. 14). Timothy needs to be wary of him as well (v. 15).

Paul's attitude toward Christians who flaked on him was quite different. At Paul's first defense, a number of Paul's colleagues ditched him. Paul asks, in their case, that it *not* be laid to their charge (v. 16). This is a response to be expected, as long as people are people. When the going gets tough, the tough get going, as the proverb has it, but those who are not tough also get going—in another direction entirely. When this happens, it is tempting for the Christians with a backbone to dismiss those who flake, and to heap contempt on them. They treat the weak as though they were in the same position as Alexander the coppersmith. But that is not Paul's response at all. He sees their desertion, and he notes the problem with it. He is not whitewashing anything, or explaining it away. But at the same time, he was praying to God to not lay it to their charge. This kind of desertion comes with the territory.

But though co-workers might leave, and fellow believers might keep their distance, Paul rejoiced that God did not leave him. God strengthened him, and the gospel was plainly set forth (v. 17). Paul was delivered from the lion's mouth, and was still around to pray for those who had abandoned him. And Paul knew that God would always do in the future what He had done in the past, delivering him from every evil work, and bringing him safely into His heavenly kingdom (v. 18). And when Paul was finally beheaded, that was not an instance of God failing him, but rather the culmination of all His faithfulness. Paul was brought into the glorious heavenly kingdom, and it did not happen too soon at all.

> Salute Prisca and Aquila, and the household of Onesiphorus. Erastus abode at Corinth: but Trophimus

have I left at Miletum sick. Do thy diligence to come before winter. Eubulus greeteth thee, and Pudens, and Linus, and Claudia, and all the brethren. The Lord Jesus Christ be with thy spirit. Grace be with you. Amen. (2 Tim. 4: 19–22)

Paul concludes by asking that greetings be extended in his name, and he passes on greetings from others. He asks Timothy to greet Priscilla and Aquila, who are apparently still at Ephesus, their old stomping ground (Acts 18:19). He also extends greetings to the household of Onesiphorus. He then mentions why he isn't sending greetings from Erastus or Trophimus, neither of whom were still with Paul. Erastus had stayed in Corinth, and Paul had left Trophimus sick in Miletus. This last little bit of news lets us know that the apostolic power of healing was not something that they had on tap. That kind of authority did mark an apostle (2 Cor. 12:12), but it was also not something they carried around with them as a personal benefit. Paul had not healed Trophimus and had left him in Miletus. He also asks Timothy to come to visit him before winter. And then he wraps up by sending greetings from Eubulus, Pudens, Linus, Claudius, and all the brothers. Fellowship extends, and should extend, over great distances. Paul then ends by giving a blessing—the Lord be with your spirit—and concludes by extending grace. The great apostle of grace bestows grace in this final word.

TITUS

INITIAL GREETING

The epistle to Titus comes from the same period of Paul's life as his two letters to Timothy, and so similarities should not be surprising. But Timothy was in Ephesus and Titus in Crete, and they had differing personalities, gifts, and challenges, so we should not be surprised by the differences between the letters.

> Paul, a servant of God, and an apostle of Jesus Christ, according to the faith of God's elect, and the acknowledging of the truth which is after godliness; In hope of eternal life, which God, that cannot lie, promised before the world began; But hath in due times manifested his word through preaching, which is committed unto me according to the commandment of God our Saviour; To

> Titus, mine own son after the common faith: Grace, mer-
> cy, and peace, from God the Father and the Lord Jesus
> Christ our Saviour. (Titus 1:1–4)

Paul calls himself a servant of God here, which stands in sharp contrast to Paul's usual "servant of Christ Jesus" (cf. Rom. 1:1), which some might take as revealing the hand of an imitator. However, if it is an imitation, it's a poor one. One of the things that an imitator would do, or so it seems to me, is *copy,* not innovate.

The phrase can be taken to mean Paul's total status before God, his apostleship being just one facet of his servanthood. In calling himself an apostle of Jesus Christ, Paul certainly didn't make the distinction between Pauline Christianity and Christ's Christianity, as so many today are inclined to do. He considered himself "sent out," a representative of the risen Christ, not a representative of Paul's own innovations.

He is laboring "according to the faith of God's elect, and the acknowledging of the truth which is after godliness." These things are not subject to his apostleship; his apostleship is subject to them. Note that "acknowledging of the truth" is only one side of the coin; it needs to go together with godliness. Truth without godliness is just so many dry bones, whether or not they are arranged in a way that is anatomically correct. Too many are led to suppose that "sound doctrine" brings godliness with it as an automatic fringe benefit. But to paraphrase William Gurnall, it is possible to have a sound head and a rotten heart.

How is this servanthood, this apostleship, to be conducted? With what motivation and what attitude? It is undertaken "in hope of eternal life." Not only does Paul hope for eternal life, his job as an apostle is to make this hope of eternal life more widespread—it is to be extended to others.

Is this hope solidly grounded or is it in the same category as the hope of winning the Lotto? No, Paul answers, this hope is built on nothing less than the character of God. God is trustworthy (not like men) and has promised. This is staked on His trustworthiness.

God promised all this "before the world began." The early fathers take this as meaning before the created order existed, God made His promise. This is most likely the case; the Greek is explicit. Some, however, prefer to translate the phrase as "ages ago" (e.g., NASB), referring to the promises given to Old Testament saints. If the former translation is accepted (as I feel it must be), then it is an indication in Scripture that time is a part of the created order and not something that God is subject to. It is subject to God: He promised eternal life before it began (cf. Eph. 1:4). Time is a creature.

God does things when He decides to do them, not when we think that it is high time God did something. God manifests His Word in due time. The New Testament emphasis on "word" is fascinating. Although God the Father is transcendent, He makes Himself manifest in the visible image of His Son, the Word. So, then, our preaching consists of words, which represents the Word, who in turn represents the Father.

God's Word is His Son, made plain in the duties of proclamation that were entrusted to Paul. Yet as that Word is
revealed to others, the body of Christ grows through proclamation. The kingdom of God does not spread in the same
manner as measles. It grows and spreads because the gospel is being preached. Also, this proclamation is valuable
and so it is important that the message be unaltered. We
can see this in the fact that the message was *entrusted* to
Paul. Only valuables are entrusted. Too many today betray
that trust given to them in the name of Christ. They mess
with the message and tinker with the gospel, hoping to
make improvements.

Taking the message to a perishing world is not optional for the Christian. This is all in accordance with the
command of God our Savior. We are entrusted with the
message and commanded to proclaim it. This phrase also
carries an implicit reference to the Deity of Christ. In this
verse, Paul uses the phrase "God our Savior." Compare this
with the phrase in the next verse, "Lord Jesus Christ our
Savior" (v. 4).

Titus was a genuine son—as opposed to some Paul could
mention. Think of Demas, who deserted Paul and revealed
his true character. Love for the world comes out at some
point. When Paul refers to Titus as "my true child in a common faith" (ESV), there are two possibilities. First, that Paul
led Titus to the Lord and is here referring to him as a true
child (of mine) in the faith. The other possibility is that Paul
is stating that Titus is a real Christian, a true child (of the
Father). I would argue for the former (cf. Gal. 2:1, 3).

Not only did Paul and Titus have access to the same God, they held that it was an access obtained through their common faith (and only through the common faith). There is only one mediator between God and man. The implication here is that if it is possible for me to share in a common faith with someone else, it follows that I don't share a part in the uncommon faiths of others. This is not religious snobbery, it is simply a desire to make clear distinctions.

Grace, mercy, and peace come from God the Father and from the Lord Jesus Christ our Savior. The Holy Spirit is not here mentioned as a *giver* of grace and mercy and peace because He *is* the gift of grace and mercy and peace. Paul deviates from his usual practice of referring to Christ as "Jesus Christ our Lord." He is making a major point by referring to Him as our Savior. It is no accident that in the two other places in this letter where he calls Christ the Savior (2:13; 3:6), he does so in close proximity to places where he has called *God* our Savior. According to Paul, Jesus is God. Not a limited Lord, or a personal Jesus, but Lord of the Universe.

LEADERSHIP QUALIFICATIONS

For this cause left I thee in Crete, that thou shouldest set in order the things that are wanting, and ordain elders in every city, as I had appointed thee: If any be blameless, the husband of one wife, having faithful children not accused of riot or unruly. For a bishop must be blameless, as the steward of God; not self-willed, not soon angry, not given to wine, no striker, not given to filthy lucre; But a lover of hospitality, a lover of good men, sober, just, holy, temperate; Holding fast the faithful word as he hath been taught, that he may be able by sound doctrine both to exhort and to convince the gainsayers. For there are many unruly and vain talkers and deceivers, specially they of the circumcision: Whose mouths must be stopped, who subvert whole houses, teaching things which they ought not, for filthy lucre's sake. One of themselves, even a prophet of their own, said, the Cretians are alway liars, evil beasts, slow bellies. This witness is true. Wherefore rebuke them sharply, that they may be sound in the faith; Not giving heed to Jewish fables, and commandments of men, that turn from the truth. Unto the pure all things are pure: but unto them that are defiled and unbelieving is nothing pure; but even their mind and conscience is defiled. They profess that they know God; but in works they deny him, being abominable, and disobedient, and unto every good work reprobate. (Titus 1:5–16)

When Paul says "for this cause I left thee in Crete," this seems to imply that Paul had been in Crete, but apparently not for long. If he had been there an extended time, it is certain that he would have taken care of all these problems himself. This is probably not his visit to Crete recorded in Acts 27, and it would therefore seem best to date the visit after the first Roman captivity.

The charge that Titus set what remained "in order" indicates that the Church in Crete was in pretty sad shape. The solution Paul proposed, or at least the first step toward the solution, was to appoint elders for each town. It looks like the entire burden of this job rested on Titus' shoulders. So then we see that there was a dearth of responsible leadership in Crete, and it was Titus' job to come up with some responsible leadership. This leadership was not to be in a central location but spread about, in every city. Titus was not to pick these elders by random choice; they had to meet Paul's particular specifications, as Paul had directed. Titus was one man responsible for the Churches of that region, and he had this authority as an apostolic emissary.

Turning to the qualifications for these elders, it looks like Paul's standards are pretty high. He begins by saying that an elder needs to be blameless, "above reproach" (ESV) (v. 6). As he required in 1 Timothy, an elder must be a one-woman man. Although this looks like a reference to polygamy, it probably is not—although it certainly would apply to polygamy. Since polygamy at that point in history was exceedingly rare, this is most likely a reference to a man who sexually dedicated and faithful.

An elder's children should be faithful believers (v. 6). An elder is responsible for evangelism in the community, and if he is not capable of leading his own children to Christ, then why would he be equipped to lead anyone else to the Lord? And if his own children were not walking with the Lord, then why should he be entrusted to lead the Church in its walk with the Lord? His children should not be charged with riot ("debauchery," ESV) or being unruly. Although this phrase refers to the children and not the father, it certainly would apply to the father. A father who does not possess the qualities required to keep his children in line also does not have the qualities required to keep the Church together.

An overseer is God's steward; a bishop is to be blameless as God's administrator (remember, "bishop" and "overseer" are the two translations the KJV and ESV use for the same word). Paul here gives a reason for these character qualifications. The elder is a representative of God; he is God's administrator, just as Paul was God's messenger or apostle. In the secular world, a representative or ambassador does his best to portray the person or country he represents. In the same way, God's administrator must administer the Church the way God Himself would. This is not just during office hours, but is round the clock.

Having made this point, Paul adds to the list. A man with these responsibilities must not be self-willed. This is a central characteristic of all godliness, the willingness to surrender our wills to the Father's will *all the time*. Our best example of this is Jesus in the garden before His death for us. He subordinated His will to the Father's will—He was not self-willed.

An elder must not be "soon angry." We read about the wrath of God in Scripture. God does get angry but He never flies off the handle. Thin-skinned elders are poor representatives of Him.

An elder does not have to be a teetotaler, but he must not be a drunkard—given to much wine. He is also not to be a bully; it is all too easy for a person in an office with authority to fall in love with that authority, instead of loving what godly authority can *do*.

An elder must not be fond of dishonest gain. When God gives His word, as we saw in v. 2, He is good for it. The elder may not be dishonest, he may not be greedy, and he may not combine the two. This concludes Paul's discussion of excluded vices and sets the stage for him to discuss pastoral virtues.

An elder must be a lover of hospitality; he must care for visitors on behalf of the Christian community, and he must model that hospitality for the congregation. He must love good men and what is good; the elder must not be chained to what is good merely by a sense of duty. He must love it for its own sake. If he is prudent, this is in contrast to the disorderly characteristics mentioned previously. He must be just, and he must be just and holy in his relations both to God and to man. These same two qualities are set alongside each other elsewhere (1 Thess. 2:10). He is to exhibit self-control (temperance), which is listed as one aspect of the fruit of the Spirit (Gal. 5:23).

He must "hold fast" to the faithful word. The word of God is faithful to us, so the least we can do is to be faithful to it. The elder is not to charge off into his own interpretations, he is to follow the apostles' teaching, he is to follow the "trustworthy word" (ESV) *as he was taught* (v. 9). This is as binding on Christian ministers today as it was in the first century. It is not a matter of whether a teaching is modern or not, but rather a matter of whether a teaching or doctrine is faithful or not. The reason for this is so that the minister might be able to exhort in sound doctrine, not to mention rebuking (ESV) those who contradict it.

The minister must be equipped to build up those who faithfully follow the Lord. This verse seems to indicate that an elder who was unfaithful to the faithful word would be unable to build up the congregation. He would also be unable to eliminate or rebuke error, since he himself had fallen into error.

When it says that those who contradict are to be rebuked, this runs contrary to the spirit of the age. Many today regard tolerance as the supreme virtue, a virtue more important than truth, any truth. While a Christian should always be gracious when he disagrees with others, there are times when he not only may take issue but where he *must* take issue. This is part of the minister's job, and in order to refute error, a minister must remain steadfast in the truth.

This is necessary because there are a lot of unruly people, vain talkers and deceivers (v. 10). The Christian faith is not only a religion, not only a relationship, it is also a discipline, a *way*. Like swimming upstream, if you stop, you are moving in the wrong direction. People who refuse that discipline, God's discipline, are undisciplined. They are idle talkers and deceivers. It doesn't take much work to come up with wrong answers. And it also doesn't take much work to deceive people with those wrong answers. In their flight from God's grace, many people *want* to be deceived.

Paul has a particular group in mind; he says "specially they of the circumcision party." These false teachers were native Cretans (v. 12), and most were of the opinion that subscription to the Mosaic Law was required for salvation.

This, along with Gnosticism, was one of the major points of danger for the first-century Church.

The ESV has Paul say "they must be silenced," but the original presents quite a vigorous picture. We might render it as "whom it would behoove to shut up," which preserves the strength of the Greek. The verb literally means to put a muzzle on an animal's mouth. This is absolutely necessary because they are a menace. They are a menace to "whole houses," and are extremely disruptive. The verb here means they "are turning things upside down." These are topsy-turvy teachers. The affected households are not having minor difficulties; these false teachers are really having a destructive impact. This is why it is so necessary to appoint qualified elders in each town.

These false teachers are presenting what they "ought not" (v. 11). They are teaching things they shouldn't, and they are doing it for "filthy lucre's sake" (v. 11), for the sake of base profit. These are not teachers who are teaching the wrong things, but with right motives. They are not merely misguided. They teach bad doctrine with impure motives. They are not honestly mistaken.

One of their own countrymen was on to them. One of the Cretans, "a prophet of their own," said that they were liars, evil beasts, slow bellies. According to Clement of Alexandria (Strom 1.59.2), the poet in question was Epimenides of Cnossus, in Crete, who was a worker of wonders and a religious teacher of the sixth century B.C. The first part of the phrase occurs in the *Hymn to Zeus*, written by Callimachus, and some have, as a result, credited him with originating it (c. 305– c. 240 B.C.). However, it is more likely that he was merely quoting the already proverbial phrase. It is interesting that Paul calls Epimenides a prophet, drawing attention to the *authority* of his judgment.

In the ancient world, Crete had a notorious reputation. The verb "to Cretize" (Grk. *kretizein*) was slang for cheating or lying. This expression is obviously meant to be taken proverbially and not strictly applied. Otherwise, how could Titus find elders who were "blameless" (v. 6)? Or if Epimenides was a Cretan, and it is true that they are always liars, then it is false because Epimenides didn't lie to us in this particular instance...and if he did, we have no reason for believing that either. In other words, Paul is not saying that no Cretan can be godly, as can be seen from his following instruction.

He confesses that Epimenides was right, but not necessarily right. Something can be done about it. Paul endorses the statement as true, *generally* true. Paul wants Titus to rebuke the Cretans sharply, so that they will be sound in the faith. It must therefore be possible for Cretans to be sound in the faith; Crete is not a lost cause. Something can be done about it. Otherwise, why have a missionary effort in Crete at all? It is possible for a Cretan to be a solid Christian. He simply must fight his culture more (in this respect) than others might have to. That is all Paul is saying here. Just as different personalities have different temptations, so also do different cultures.

With the next phrase, "not giving heed to Jewish fables" (v. 14), we get some light on the nature of this particular heresy. The Jewish fables very likely have strong similarities to the fables mentioned in 1 Tim. 1:4, although they are designated as peculiarly Jewish here. The "commandments" mentioned here cannot be the Mosaic law because, for Paul, the Old Testament was God-given. Given the broader context, it is likely that he is talking about Jewish/Gnostic ascetic rules and regulations, e.g., bans on particular foods, along with marriage (1 Tim. 4:3–6). It is interesting that the similar tendencies in the Colossian heresy are also referred to as "commandments of men" (Col. 2:21 ff.)

And it is not that these men have never encountered the truth. Rather, they have met the truth face to face and have turned away.

All is clean to the clean. For the pure, "all things are pure" (v. 15). We see in this context Paul is talking about the things that these teachers would like to forbid. He is *not* saying, for example, that to the pure fornication or adultery would be clean. God forbid. He is saying that to the clean, all banned foods are clean. But to the defiled and unbelieving ones, everything is corrupted. Nothing is clean. For the false teachers that Paul is dealing with here nothing is pure. They are like a driver who has mud all over his windshield and assumes that the scenic countryside is filthy. They declare *other* things unclean because they are unclean. They now have trouble distinguishing right and wrong. The pollution is of the inner man.

They claim to know God, but they do not. They affirm Him with their mouths, but deny Him with their works. The kingdom of God does not consist in words but in power. We are not to love with words only, but in deed and truth. Faith without works is dead. Despite their profession, they are abominable, disobedient, and unfit (ESV) for anything worthwhile. The first adjective here is really strong. As a noun, it means "abomination." Their disobedience is exhibited by their refusal to obey the word of God, their refusal of grace, and their denial of the goodness of the creation. They stand in sharp contrast to the "man of God" in 2 Tim. 3:17, who *is* equipped for every good work. These teachers destroy their moral ability with their false systems taught with impure motives.

IN LINE WITH SOUND DOCTRINE

But speak thou the things which become sound doctrine: That the aged men be sober, grave, temperate, sound in faith, in charity, in patience. The aged women likewise, that they be in behaviour as becometh holiness, not false accusers, not given to much wine, teachers of good things; That they may teach the young women to be sober, to love their husbands, to love their children, To be discreet, chaste, keepers at home, good, obedient to their own husbands, that the word of God be not blasphemed. Young men likewise exhort to be sober minded. In all things shewing thyself a pattern of good works: in doctrine shewing uncorruptness, gravity, sincerity, Sound speech, that cannot be condemned; that he that is of the contrary part may be ashamed, having no evil thing to say of you. Exhort servants to be obedient unto their own masters, and to please them well in all things; not answering again; Not purloining, but shewing all good fidelity; that they may adorn the doctrine of God our Saviour in all things. (Titus 2:1–10)

The false teachers were leading people astray, and Titus was to prevent that. How? He was to counter it with sound doctrine, with healthy teaching. There is no question that for Paul correct belief and correct behavior are linked closely together. Healthy teaching is implicitly contrasted with the diseased teaching of the false teachers. Paul does not merely denounce the heresy, he gives the antidote—which is sound teaching. It is not the case that teaching is simply a matter of transferring propositions. Solid teaching is the appropriate response to people who want to live in a way that denies God by their works.

As befits the elderly in any community, the older Christian men are to command respect. They are to be temperate, not self-indulgent. Their seriousness is not to be confused with gloominess. And they should have a handle on themselves; they are not to be out of control. But in many communities, older non-Christians are often expected to fit this description. Thus Paul adds a little more—they are to be sound in the faith, in love and in patience. This is a specific Christian touch. A man who walks with the Lord finds his faith getting stronger with age, not the reverse. His love should counteract the natural tendency of the elderly to be censorious or to find fault. His patience should simply reinforce this. It is interesting that patience is substituted for hope in this particular triad. Instead of faith, hope and love we find faith, patience, and love.

All this character emphasis for the elderly is not limited to just the men. Older women are to be "in behavior as becometh holiness," a catch-all phrase which would touch all areas of their lives, including what is subsequently and specifically mentioned in the following list. The older women are to be godly, period. What might that mean when we push it into the corners? First, they are not to be false accusers. These women are *not* to allow the tendency to talk about others in a harmful way to get control of their conversations. All too often we would rather repeat bad than good of a person. They are not to be "given to much wine." The word "given" is connected with slavery here, and is much stronger than the word used in 1 Timothy. Paul warned Titus earlier about Cretan culture, and the failings of slander and drunkenness in the older women would be part of that.

The older women must be taught in such a way that they may in turn teach what is good. Again, Paul does not simply warn against the bad, he gives the antidote, which is good teaching. The older women are to be taught what is good so that they might teach what is good to the younger women. When the younger women learn these things early on, they are that much more ahead of the game. Nowhere does Paul teach that women are not to teach. He does insist that women should not teach or have authority over men, but he expects that women who have the wisdom and the gifts should teach other women.

Specifically, the older women are to teach younger women how to be husband-lovers and children-lovers. A colloquial rendering would say that the younger women need to be taught to be into their husbands and into their kids. This is especially necessary in our day.

There are two points to be made here. The first is that these twin virtues were regarded as the glory of young womanhood for both Jews and pagans. Paul insists on this so that the word of God would not be reviled. The only place where that would happen would be among the pagan outsiders, or among the unbelieving Jews.

The second point is that familial love is a discipline, a vocation that must be learned. This might strike many as odd, thinking that such family relationships should develop naturally, all by themselves. But for Paul, the type of love that God wants wives to cultivate toward their husbands and children *must be taught.* The ones who are equipped to do the teaching are godly older women, who have lived out this vocation themselves. Godly older women are necessary if the younger women are to become apprentices.

What follows then is the content of what the younger women should be taught. First, they are to be discreet (KJV) or self-controlled (ESV). It would not be far off to call Titus the epistle of self-control; Paul mentions it often. Again, this might be a major indicator of what Crete was like, not exactly a bastion of self-control. Paul also wants the young women to be taught purity (v. 4). These first two requirements might be a referral to their sex lives. The young women are to be pure and chaste and in control of themselves.

The younger women are also to be taught to be industrious at home, "keepers at home." Paul emphasizes the importance of women being given to the domestic arts. Many like to think that Paul is simply reflecting the culture of his day, as opposed to reflecting God's standards on the matter. The problem is that Paul does not make this distinction. Also, why are we asked to believe that Paul was so enslaved by his culture that he could not distinguish between it and the word of God, while at the same time we are asked to believe that these modern and very liberal interpreters of Paul are somehow marvelously free from their culture? How did that happen? I'd rather trust Paul, who had a much better record when it came to swimming against the tide.

They are to be kind women (v. 4, ESV), and obedient to their own husbands. If the Bible is the Word of God, and it is, then we need to recognize that submission of a wife to her husband is clearly taught there. The reason for this household order is so that the Word of God not be reviled. These principles of family discipline are to be strictly followed. When they are not followed, families fall apart. And when Christian homes are in shambles, the word of God is slandered.

Again, this is the epistle of self-control. The young men are urged to be self-controlled as well (v. 5). This requirement is not limited by sex. Both sexes, both old and young, are called to be godly and self-controlled. The imperative is used for the first time here; Paul's language is getting stronger.

It is not clear whether the phrase "in all things" goes with the previous command to the young men, or with the injunction to Titus which follows. The KJV applies it to the command to Titus. Titus was told to show himself, in all things, a pattern of good works. Titus is not to lay all these requirements on others without fulfilling them himself. Titus is called to practice what he preaches. If Titus wants an effective ministry, his life must back up his words, and be a showcase for them. To paraphrase Jonathan Edwards, "It's easier to get 'em to talk like saints than to act like saints."

He is to work out what is good. His *actions* are to be in order. He is to be a doer of the word. Paul then turns from the actions of the preacher to his words. He says, "In doctrine show . . . ." His words must not only be correct, but they also must be said with a proper attitude—"uncorruptness, gravity, sincerity, sound speech." Titus must not be flippant. Christianity is serious business, but this does not mean gloomy. It is not careless or slipshod. The preacher doesn't have to be glum, but he must not be frivolous or frothy.

Sound speech is healthy speech, and it is beyond reproach. It cannot be condemned. Healthy speech is conducive to the apostolic gospel, the gospel of grace through faith. But this speech must be uttered in such a way that no one can find problems with the attitude. This advice is practical in that it robs the enemy of the Church a weapon which could be used against her. Titus is to speak in such a way that an opponent will be ashamed, having nothing evil to say about the Church (v. 8).

The gospel governs all social relations, and this includes social relations that began in sin, like slavery. But the gospel also addresses the sinfulness of such relations from top to bottom—there is no assumption that the only sin possible is on the side of the masters. The institution is subverted by teaching slaves to be submissive to their own masters in everything. Paul is probably talking about household slaves here ("servants" in the KJV), but the teaching would apply across the board. The instruction to slaves here is stronger than similar injunctions in Ephesians and Colossians. Again, this could be in response to the conditions unique to Cretan culture. Cretan slaves were perhaps a bit more mouthy, and so they are told not to be argumentative (ESV). They are to please their masters well, as a testimony to their masters (Christian or not) with their behavior. They are to try to please their masters, and not talk back. Since what comes out of the mouth is a good indication of what is in the heart, these slaves are being required to keep their attitudes straight.

The slave is not to steal from his master; he is not to pilfer anything. Neither is he to abuse any privilege. The irony is that a Christian slave (who is property) is being required here to respect his master's property. This—for those who understand the logic of the gospel—subverts the institution of slavery in ways that insolence and pilfering could not. A Christian slave should be an honest, trustworthy slave. Why is this? This is done in order to adorn the doctrine of the gospel. This kind of demeanor makes the gospel attractive, and when that happens, the old system is upended as men come to Christ. No one is attracted to Christ through manifestly ungodly Christians. Our job as Christians is to live out the teachings of Jesus in order that the world can indeed see the full attractiveness of them. The verb here is used in the arrangement of jewels so that their full beauty may be clearly seen. So it is with us.

GRACE NOW MANIFESTED

For the grace of God that bringeth salvation hath appeared to all men, Teaching us that, denying ungodliness and worldly lusts, we should live soberly, righteously, and godly, in this present world; Looking for that blessed

hope, and the glorious appearing of the great God and
our Saviour Jesus Christ; Who gave himself for us, that
he might redeem us from all iniquity, and purify unto
himself a peculiar people, zealous of good works. These
things speak, and exhort, and rebuke with all authority.
Let no man despise thee. (Titus 2:11–15)

The grace of God is now manifest, and it brings salvation for
everybody. This grace is nothing other than the birth, death,
and resurrection of Jesus Christ. Our salvation by grace is
completely and utterly dependent on Him. All men have
knowledge of God's grace to some degree, or at least of God's
character. God is not narrow, as some would make Him out
to be—His salvation is offered to everyone. And though He
has one means of salvation (the gospel of Christ), that does
not make this offer narrow. The fact that there is only one
bridge across a great river does not mean that the one bridge
is a narrow one. That is a different issue entirely.

God's grace not only saves us, it teaches us (v. 12). Not
only does God save us from the *penalty* of sin, He also desires to save us from the *power* of sin. God's saving activity
has a disciplinary aspect. There is also a double injunction—the negative is followed by the positive. We must
deny ungodliness and worldly lusts in the first place, but
we are not to stop there. We are also to live self-controlled
lives, lives that are righteous and godly. Again, notice the
emphasis on self-control. Having denied what is wrong,
believers are now to affirm the right. How? With their
lives. These righteous and godly lives are not just to be
lived in the sweet by-and-by, but here and now, in this

present age. This present age stands in sharp contrast to the event mentioned in the next verse.

We live a certain way now, expecting the blessed hope to come (v. 13). We are to live in this age (ESV), all the while looking forward to the next age. What is this blessed hope? Paul's answer is that it is the "appearing of the glory of our great God and Savior Jesus Christ" (ESV). This is where the two previously mentioned streams in Titus converge. Before this, the deity of Christ is strongly alluded to, but here it comes out explicitly. At the end of this present age, God *Himself* will appear in the person of Jesus Christ. The KJV and some translations blunt this point by translating it as something like "the great God *and* our Savior Christ Jesus." There is more than one problem with this. There is no grammatical reason for making a separation. And there are no parallels in the New Testament that refer to God as "great," or God as "appearing." Instead of looking for reasons to be suspicious that early scribes were looking to deify Christ, perhaps we should instead reflect on the possibility that some modern scholars might want to deny it. But for Paul, Jesus is very definitely God. This phrase is likely an excerpt from an early Christian hymn or liturgy.

Jesus gave Himself for us in order to redeem us. This may be paraphrased as "Jesus loves me this I know, for the Bible tells me so." He gave Himself in order to redeem us from all iniquity. The language here is likely a paraphrase from Ps. 79:8. The active force of that redemption was the blood of Jesus Christ (1 Jn. 1:7). Once we have been brought out of that lawless iniquity, we are made part of the people of God. God's intent was to purify us for

Himself, a people for His own possession (ESV), and who are zealous for good works.

Speak these things, Paul says (v. 15). This is in the imperative; it is *not* optional (cf. 2:1). Titus should not only declare the message, but exhort his charges to follow him. Not only that, but he is also to reprove those who do not listen to him, and he must do it with all authority. When a preacher sets absolute standards which the people would rather not have, he might run into resistance. Thus, Titus is not to let anybody despise him.

FREE GRACE AND GOOD WORKS

> Put them in mind to be subject to principalities and powers, to obey magistrates, to be ready to every good work, To speak evil of no man, to be no brawlers, but gentle, shewing all meekness unto all men. For we ourselves also were sometimes foolish, disobedient, deceived, serving divers lusts and pleasures, living in malice and envy, hateful, and hating one another. But after that the kindness and love of God our Saviour toward man appeared, Not by works of righteousness which we have done, but according to his mercy he saved us, by the washing of regeneration, and renewing of the Holy Ghost; Which he shed on us abundantly through Jesus Christ our Saviour; That being justified by his grace, we should be made heirs according to the hope of eternal life. (Titus 3:1–7)

Thus far Paul has been concerned with internal relations in the Cretan Church, with how Christians should deal with fellow Christians. This has an impact on the outside world (in terms of testimony), but he now moves to the subject of direct relationship of the Christians to governmental authorities.

This relationship exists for two reasons. First, governmental authority stems from God. If God has established civil government, then Christians should be in a right relationship to it. And secondly, in line with an emphasis throughout the book, Christians need to be concerned with the impression they make on the outside world. If the Christians behave as scofflaws, the gospel could very easily be discredited by the association.

Christians must be *obedient* to the civil authorities. This needs very little clarification. Everything else being equal, we are to obey the government. When Paul says we are to be ready "for every good work" (v. 1), it is unlikely that this is referring to specifically Christian acts of charity. Given the context, this is more likely an exhortation for Christians to get involved in the kind of work that goes with good citizenship.

We are not to speak evil of anyone. We must avoid slander, not saying anything unless it is true, loving, and necessary. We are to avoid brawling (quarreling, ESV), and must be peaceable. Christians are not to pick fights with non-Christians. While the Christian is involved in spiritual warfare, true enough, the enemy is Satan and *not* non-believers. Non-believers are the contested territory; they are what the war is *over*. So as far as it is possible with the Christians, peace should be the norm. Paul adds to this the requirement of gentleness. This does not betray weakness.

Jesus was gentle and yet had the authority to cleanse the Temple. We make a mistake when we separate gentleness and authority. We are to show all meekness ("perfect courtesy," ESV) to everyone (v. 2). This would include those who are hostile to the gospel, not just to those who happen to be personal friends or fellow Christians.

Why is this? We should be thoughtful of them, because we used to be just like them. We were ourselves "sometimes foolish" (v. 3). We were disobedient ourselves, and led astray. We were under a deception, which ought to make us considerate of those in a similar plight. Non-believers, in their blindness to the reality of God and His law, are fools. They are also disobedient, belligerent to true authority. They have also allowed false guides to lead them off the right track, men who are slaves to various passions and pleasures. Of course, pleasure is possible in disobedience to God, but apart from Him, the pleasures curdle quickly. God does not mind us having pleasure; He minds pleasure having us. He prohibits us having pleasure apart from Him. And the only way to keep pleasure pure is to subject oneself to God's moral law.

When we were like to them, we lived in malice and envy, which contaminated whatever pleasures we did possess. For outside God's standard, apart from His law, pleasure cannot remain *true* pleasure. Corrupted in that way, we were hateful and spent our time hating one another. But the loveliness of Christ is such that, apart from Him, no loveliness remains. His loveliness is complete.

When Jesus Christ became man, it was out of a love for mankind and a true kindness toward mankind on the part of God. The goodness and loving kindness (toward us) appeared in the world. We may rest in the fact that God does not play games with us. He cared enough to become one of us.

He saved us (v. 5). Paul goes on to say that the Incarnation was not a miracle to no purpose. God undertook to become a man in order to accomplish our salvation. The verb here is in the aorist tense, and indicates the once-for-all nature of that salvation.

What was *not* the basis of this settled salvation? It was certainly not because of anything *we* did—"Not by works of righteousness which we have done." Any lingering doubts about Pauline authorship should shipwreck on this rock. Salvation does not now and never did depend on the credit entries we think we have racked up in the heavenly ledgers. It is according to His own mercy, pure and simple.

Our salvation is through the "washing of regeneration," and the "renewal of the Holy Ghost." Our salvation has two aspects. One is the foundational restoration. We are quickened; we are regenerated. And then the sanctifying renewal of the Holy Spirit begins. This all begins at conversion. This may be an excerpt from an early baptismal hymn. Not only would the early Christians enact the gospel in the ritual of water baptism, they would also sing about it.

When God gives ordinary gifts, He doesn't hold back. Should we think He would do less with His wonderful gift of the Holy Spirit? The Holy Spirit is poured out on us "abundantly" (v. 6). This figure of "pouring out" is used in Acts 2:17, which is itself a fulfillment of Joel 2:28. How is all this accomplished? Paul answers that it happens "through Jesus Christ our Savior." God does not indiscriminately pour out His Spirit on people who are unaffected by it. He is the *Holy* Spirit, and sin will be dealt with. A holy God cannot leave people in the midst of all their immoralities without doing something. When God saves us from drowning, He does not leave us on the bottom of the pool.

Justification is not only for the here and now, it provides the basis for looking forward to the next age. Now having our heads above water, we can look about for land. We look forward to the culmination of this gift. We have become heirs according to the hope of eternal life. This is what we have to look forward to—nothing less than eternal life. Since it is still in the future, it is referred to as a hope. In Romans 8:17 and Galatians 4:7, adopted sons are referred to as heirs of eternal life. Elsewhere in the New Testament, we are referred to as joint-heirs with Christ.

> This is a faithful saying, and these things I will that thou affirm constantly, that they which have believed in God might be careful to maintain good works. These things are good and profitable unto men. But avoid foolish questions, and genealogies, and contentions, and strivings about the law; for they are unprofitable and vain. A man that is an heretic after the first and second admonition reject; Knowing that he that is such is subverted, and sinneth, being condemned of himself. (Titus 3:8–11)

This word is faithful. The saying is trustworthy. This is one of Paul's favorite expressions in the Pastorals; he is wanting to pass down wisdom in memorable form. This probably refers to what went before: Paul wants Titus to insist on these things (v. 8). This truth of justification is to be insisted on. Compromise at this point is compromise at a vital point. Luther stated it well when he said that justification is the article of a standing or falling Church. Why is this? Everything—true conversion and the resultant Christian life depend on it. Free grace and free justification are no enemy to good works; they are the only possible foundation of true good works.

Those who have believed in God are to be careful to do good works. Those who have believed in good works cannot do them. Those who reject good works, and who trust in Christ, are then able to *devote* themselves to good works. When you get basic doctrine under your belt, you then have your hands free to get involved in good works. This is why it is essential to insist on justification by grace alone through faith alone. This is not done so that we will spend all our time on that doctrine, but rather to enable us to go on. This is profitable for others. Men are benefited by what we do and say, and not just by what we say.

By way of contrast, Paul says we are to stay out of foolish questions (or controversies, ESV) (v. 9). We are not to get tangled up in genealogies. Nor are we to participate in contentions or in strivings about the law. Why? They don't accomplish anything. The Greek word for *avoid* here means "face the other way." Have *nothing* to do with these things because they are useless and vain. It is not always smart to fight fire with fire. Paul is instructing Titus *not* to descend to the level of the heresy. Leave it be. This is not a time to answer a fool according to his folly.

As for the fellow who stirs up division, he should get one or two admonitions (v. 10). After that, if he does not mend, have nothing to do with him. This is not to say that there is never any room for disagreements—but someone who disagrees just for the sake of disagreement, *this* is the man to avoid. The Greek word here provides the root for our term heretic (which is how the KJV translates it), but there is no reason to think that is the type of person Paul is referring to here. Our close association between this word and heterodox theology came in by the second century. Paul's sense here is a person who in his persistence divides believers. He is talking about a divisive man, not a false teacher. Given the kind of man we are talking about, Paul's leniency is striking. It's not as though he is booted out at the first sign of trouble. He gets two warnings before he is avoided.

This is a man who has been warped; he has turned aside. He was once on the correct path and then left it. After leaving the right path, he was warned by Church leaders at least twice and he chose to persist in his rebellion. Such a man is sinful, and has fallen short of God's glory. This person is not only condemned by God and by the Church, but he also condemns himself. Why? For the simple reason that he knows better. The representative of God's gospel of grace has warned him. So if he maintains his sin, there is no excuse. His own better judgment condemns him.

FINAL INSTRUCTIONS

> When I shall send Artemas unto thee, or Tychicus, be
> diligent to come unto me to Nicopolis: for I have de-
> termined there to winter. Bring Zenas the lawyer and
> Apollos on their journey diligently, that nothing be want-
> ing unto them. And let ours also learn to maintain good
> works for necessary uses, that they be not unfruitful. All
> that are with me salute thee. Greet them that love us in
> the faith. Grace be with you all. Amen. (Titus 3:12–15)

Paul has not yet made up his mind which of his lieu-
tenants he will send to Crete. It will either be Artemas or
Tychicus (v. 12). When he does decide, and Titus receives
them, he is to do what he can to meet with Paul at Nicopolis. This is probably Nicopolis on the Greek mainland, close
to the modern town of Pureza. Paul is probably not there
yet, but has decided to winter there. This Nicopolis is much
better situated for "wintering" than the other towns with
that name. And if, according to 2 Tim. 4:10, Titus wound
up in Dalmatia, this would fit well with him meeting Paul
in Nicopolis.

Paul seeks help for Zenas the lawyer, with this being the
only place that Zenas is mentioned. His name is Greek, and
is short for Zenodorus. This literally means "gift of Zeus."
His profession is most likely named to distinguish him from
another Zenas. Paul was also seeking help for Apollos. The
chances are good that this is the eloquent Jew from Alexandria, "mighty in the Scriptures," whom we met in Acts
18:24 and who later wound up preaching at Corinth (1
Cor. 1:12). Zenas and Apollos are very likely the bearers of

this letter to Titus. They have left Paul and are traveling to parts unknown. Titus is to help them on the way, and to do so in such a way as that they want nothing. Paul is seeking not only hospitality for them, but generous hospitality.

He then returns to one of the burdens of this book. Our people should learn how to do good work constantly (v. 14). The emphasis of this whole book has been on behavior, good works, and all built on the foundation of the gospel. Paul adds another little note. This good behavior is to be all the time, and not sporadic. It is to be consistent. Neither is it to be scatter-brained. It should be well-planned and thought out.

They are to give to urgent needs, and not to false alarms. Chasing after false needs is a good way to be unfruitful, which Paul does not want at all. Too many Christians are unfruitful because they don't use their brains. Christians are to be generous in how they give money away, but this is not the same thing as throwing it out the window. Christians are to spend themselves, their time, and their money *intelligently*.

All who are with Paul send their greetings. And in the opposite direction, Paul asks Titus to greet all those in Crete who love them. Paul asks for grace to be with them all. The *you* here is plural, including the whole community. The plural could be an indication that the expectation was that the letter would be read publicly to the whole congregation, or perhaps to a series of congregations (cf. 1 Tim. 6:21; 2 Tim. 4:22).

APPENDIX:
AGE AND THE ELDERSHIP

False understandings of the etymologies of words sometimes cause minor confusion or bad jokes. Only rarely
does it cause significant problems, but one exception to
this is the difficulty caused by some Christians who believe
that only elderly men are qualified to be elders of Churches. Not only does this mean that many capable men are
excluded from leadership in the Church for most of their
lives, it also means that when some of them finally come
into the pastoral ministry, they do this as older men, but
as novices to the pastoral office. The purpose of this short
essay is to show that this assumption is misguided, and
that it works against the very thing it wants to encourage,
which is maturity in office.

Of course, the word *prebyteros*—usually translated *elder*—does carry the meaning "old man." But this is not the only meaning it carries. It can also refer to those who hold a particular office—and where the office derived its name provides us with a good example of the etymological fallacy. Where a word came from and what a word means are two different things entirely. In earlier (tribal and patriarchal) times it would have been older men who overwhelmingly would have held that office, and so it was natural that such a name would be given. But once the office and name are established, a young man can certainly step into it.

We have an exact parallel to this in our use of the word *senator*. The word is related to the Latin *senex* which means old man. The root *sen-* indicates age, and we get the words *senator, senile,* and *senior* from it. And yet obviously, a young man can be elected to office and become a senator. According to the U.S. Constitution, a senator has to be out of his twenties. "No person shall be a Senator who shall not have attained to the age of thirty years."[3] Thirty is young, but thirty can be a *senator.*

Another variation is seen in how *Thayer's Greek/English Lexicon* divides references to age signified by this word into at least three categories—the first is where two people are spoken of and one is the elder of the two (Luke 15:25). The elder brother (*prebyteros*) of the prodigal was still a young man. The second age reference is the obvious one under discussion—it refers to one advanced in life, a

3 Article I, Section 3.

senior. And yet another usage is when what we would call *forefathers* are spoken of.

So we see that the word refers to the one who holds a particular "rank or office," such as a member of the great council or Sanhedrin. The Sanhedrin was the body of elders for the nation of Israel. But there were local sanhedrins or courts as well.

> In a few cases, other words are substituted for *synedrion*, e.g., *presbyterion*, 'body of elders' (Luke xxii. 66; Acts xxii.5), and *gerousia*, 'senate' (Acts v.21) . . . The councils (*synedria*) of Mt. v. 22, x. 17; Mk. xiii. 9, and the *boulai* of Jos., *Ant.* iv. 8. 14, etc. were local courts of at least seven elders, and in large towns up to twenty-three elders.[4]

This form of local and broader government developed by the Jews was picked up and extended by the early Christian Church. Christian Churches are sometimes called synagogues (Jas. 2:2), and they certainly followed the same pattern of government (Acts 14:23). The church council in Acts 15 was a Christian Sanhedrin (Acts 15: 2,4,6,22–23).

All this is relevant because we may note the age requirements the Jews had for such office, and we may see how the Christian Church carried those requirements over. But to do so we have to piece some things together.

The Jews required that a man be thirty years old before he could be a member of the Great Sanhedrin. But thirty is comparatively young. Paul shows his membership in that body when he tells us how he *voted* in the persecution of

---

4 J.D. Douglas, ed., *New Bible Dictionary* (Grand Rapids: Eerdmans, 1962), 1142.

the Church. "I verily thought with myself, that I ought to do many things contrary to the name of Jesus of Nazareth. Which thing I also did in Jerusalem: and many of the saints did I shut up in prison, having received authority from the chief priests; and when they were put to death, I gave my voice against them" (Acts 26:9–10). The literal rendering of "gave my voice" is "cast a pebble," i.e., he is referring to a vote.

Commenting on Acts 26:10, I. Howard Marshall says that the fact that Paul voted against the Christians indicated his membership in the great Sanhedrin. "Since, however, Paul is talking about his activity in Jerusalem, membership of the supreme Sanhedrin is no doubt indicated."[5]

The interesting thing here is that we know that Paul was a young man around this time. "And cast him out of the city, and stoned him: and the witnesses laid down their clothes *at a young man's feet*, whose name was Saul" (Acts 7:58).

How young? Paul was *born* a Roman citizen, as he put it (Acts 22:27). There were two acts by Rome which established registration of citizenry at birth. The first was *lex Aelia Sentia* in 4 A.D. and the second was *lex Papia Poppaea* in 9 A.D.[6] If Stephen was martyred around A.D. 30, then this meant that Paul was likely in his mid-twenties. If he had been born before 4 A.D., then his citizenship would not have been registered at birth, so a birth date between 4 and 9 A.D. is most likely.

5 I. Howard Marshall, *Acts: Tyndale New Testament Commentaries* (Downers Grove, IL: InterVarsity Press, 1980), 393.

6 F.F. Bruce, *Paul: Apostle of the Heart Set Free* (Grand Rapids: Eerdmans, 1977), 40.

Paul had made a mark on his people from the very beginning. "My manner of life *from my youth*, which was at the first among mine own nation at Jerusalem, know all the Jews; Which knew me from the beginning, if they would testify, that after the most straitest sect of our religion I lived a Pharisee" (Acts 26:4–5). And so, although the Sanhedrin limited membership to those who were at least thirty, there may have been an exception in Paul's case. As he put it once:

> For ye have heard of my conversation in time past in the Jews' religion, how that beyond measure I persecuted the church of God, and wasted it: And profited in the Jews' religion above many my equals in mine own nation, being more exceedingly zealous of the traditions of my fathers. (Gal. 1:13–14)

Not only did Paul serve the God of Israel before his conversion to Christ at a young age, but we must also note that it was in the middle of this youthful persecution of the Church that God made him an apostle. And Paul did not consider himself an anomaly in this, but was more than willing to follow the same pattern in how he trained others for ministry. The principal example of this is the case of Timothy.

The apostle Paul died around A.D. 67 at the hands of Nero. Just before his death, he wrote his second letter to Timothy. In that letter he told Timothy to guard against *the sins of youth.* "Flee also *youthful lusts*: but follow righteousness, faith, charity, peace, with them that call on the

Lord out of a pure heart" (2 Tim. 2:22). In 1 Timothy, the point is even more explicit.

> These things command and teach. Let no man *despise thy youth*; but be thou an example of the believers, in word, in conversation, in charity, in spirit, in faith, in purity. (1 Tim. 4:11–12).

Not only are we told that Timothy is a young man here, but we are further told that it is the duty of a young minister to keep people from despising that youth, which is a natural mistake for the people to make when a *young* man is an *elder*.

But the meaning of the chronology is that we must make this point even stronger. Paul is calling Timothy a young man, one whose youth might be despised, in the mid-sixties. But Timothy had joined Paul *in ministry* about *twenty* years before. The first missionary journey occurred in the mid-forties, and Paul had probably met Timothy in the mission to Lystra and Derbe. When he came back through on the second journey, he picked Timothy up as a lieutenant in ministry (Acts 16:1–3). This means that Timothy probably joined Paul in ministry while in his mid-teens.

Timothy is still a young man (in his thirties) twenty years later, but an authority in the Church. One of his duties was to oversee the appointment of elders (1 Tim. 3:1–7), as well as handling charges that might be brought against such elders (1 Tim. 5:19). Of course, Timothy was charged to remember his youth in how he addressed and exhorted those who were his elders (1 Tim. 5:1), but he was *still* called upon to exhort them pastorally. In short, Timothy was given a significant ministerial charge while still a young man, and so we are not permitted to think that youth, by itself, presents an obstacle to ministry.

And so what should our application be? Those who are called to the ministry of the Word are often called to that vocation from their youth. Samuel first heard the word of the Lord as a boy, and in the Christian era, cases like Charles Spurgeon come to mind, who began preaching while still a teenager. My own forehead reddens to think that my first sermon was delivered in a Lutheran Church when I was seventeen years old. Somebody should have been paying closer attention than they were, but the fact remains that the call of preaching has been a weight on me since I was a small boy. Now the fact that someone is called from his youth does not mean that he should hold office from his youth. But it does mean that older saints around such a person may bring him into ministry early, and nurture him in his calling.

And so there are three points of application that I would suggest. The first is that collective maturity on a session of elders *is* desirable. While a conservative approach is to be applauded, it is important that it not be wooden. Timothy is told not to be hasty in the laying on of hands (1 Tim. 5:22), and a neophyte in the faith can cause havoc (1 Tim. 3:6). But if a session has a good number of gray heads, and a wise, collective gravity, then to bring the strength and energy of qualified young men into the context of that kind of ministry is not a *lesser* good, but rather a *higher* good.

An eldership without such young men is handicapped in some significant respects.

Second, the age of the children of elders should not be something we take into consideration by itself. This is because to do so is to go beyond the requirements of Scripture. We should see the unwieldiness of such extensions almost immediately. What about an older man with younger children? What about an older man with older daughters, and then a young son? What about a childless older man who becomes an elder, and then his wife conceives? We need to keep it simple. The Bible requires that if a man has a household, then it must be managed well, and the congregation should know that it is managed well. If a man cannot do this, then how can he manage the household of God (1 Tim. 3:5)? But this knowledge is not to be established only after eighty years.

And third, we may do all this with confidence if we have the commitment to maintain a biblical standard of qualification for all elders—to become elders in the first place according to relevant scriptural criteria, and then to maintain their position as elders after the fact, also in accordance with the appropriate scriptural criteria. If those in ministry have the commitment to maintain their qualifications in all diligence, this means that they have the commitment to step down from ministry should disarray in their household make it evident that they must do so. When this happens, it is a cause of grief, but it is also healthy for the Church, and for younger elders. A young man with young children should never view his ordination as the one hurdle he must get past, and then he is settled in the ministry for life.

In all these things, we should never forget that in the days of the new covenant, God promised to do a marvelous thing, which included young men seeing visions (Acts 2:17–18).

So when we consider the godly maturity of a board of elders, age is obviously a factor. But it is not the only factor. Age by itself is not a guarantee of maturity, and youth does not guarantee immaturity. A young man can be wise beyond his years, and older men can be foolish. Age is a natural receptacle for wisdom and maturity, and we should desire such collective wisdom and maturity for our session of elders. But an essential part of this is learning how to bring young men into ministry in such a way that fifty years from now, we will not only have elders who are eighty years old, but also have elders who have been ministering to souls for fifty of those years. A sixty-year-old man who is made an elder may be wise in his household and business, but in the ministry he is still a novice.

If we want great wine decades from now, it is important to begin laying down the bottles now.